THE COURTS

Published in association with the Centre for Canadian Studies at Mount Allison University. Information on the Canadian Democratic Audit project can be found at www.CanadianDemocraticAudit.ca.

Advisory Group

Titles

THE COURTS

Ian Greene

UBCPress

16 15 14 13 12 11 10 09 08 07 06   5 4 3 2 1

Printed in Canada on ancient-forest-free paper (100% post-consumer recycled) that is processed chlorine- and acid-free, with vegetable-based inks.

Library and Archives Canada Cataloguing in Publication

Greene, Ian
    The courts / Ian Greene.

(Canadian democratic audit; 9)
Includes bibliographical references and index.
ISBN-13: 978-0-7748-1184-2
ISBN-10: 0-7748-1184-6
ISBN-10: 0-7748-1101-3 (set)

    1. Courts – Canada. 2. Justice, Administration of – Canada. 3. Judicial power – Canada. I. Title. II. Series.

KE8200.G74 2006   347.71'01   C2005-907092-7
KF8719.G74 2006

Canadä

UBC Press gratefully acknowledges the financial support for our publishing program of the Government of Canada through the Book Publishing Industry Development Program (BPIDP), and of the Canada Council for the Arts and the British Columbia Arts Council.

The Centre for Canadian Studies thanks the Harold Crabtree Foundation for its support of the Canadian Democratic Audit project.

Copy editor: Sarah Wight
Text design: Peter Ross, Counterpunch
Typesetter: Artegraphica Design Co. Ltd.
Proofreader: Jennie Rubio
Indexer: Noeline Bridge

UBC Press
The University of British Columbia
2029 West Mall
Vancouver, BC V6T 1Z2
604-822-5959 / Fax: 604-822-6083
www.ubcpress.ca

Contents

Foreword

This volume is part of the Canadian Democratic Audit series. The objective of this series is to consider how well Canadian democracy is performing at the outset of the twenty-first century. In recent years, political and opinion leaders, government commissions, academics, citizen groups, and the popular press have all identified a "democratic deficit" and "democratic malaise" in Canada. These characterizations often are portrayed as the result of a substantial decline in Canadians' confidence in their democratic practices and institutions. Indeed, Canadians are voting in record low numbers, many are turning away from the traditional political institutions, and a large number are expressing declining confidence in both their elected politicians and the electoral process.

Nonetheless, Canadian democracy continues to be the envy of much of the rest of the world. Living in a relatively wealthy and peaceful society, Canadians hold regular elections in which millions cast ballots. These elections are largely fair, efficient, and orderly events. They routinely result in the selection of a government with no question about its legitimate right to govern. Developing democracies from around the globe continue to look to Canadian experts for guidance in establishing electoral practices and democratic institutions. Without a doubt, Canada is widely seen as a leading example of successful democratic practice.

Given these apparently competing views, the time is right for a comprehensive examination of the state of Canadian democracy. Our purposes are to conduct a systematic review of the operations of Canadian democracy, to listen to what others have to say about Canadian democracy, to assess its strengths and weaknesses, to consider where there are opportunities for advancement, and to evaluate popular reform proposals.

A democratic audit requires the setting of benchmarks for evaluation of the practices and institutions to be considered. This necessarily involves substantial consideration of the meaning of democracy.

"Democracy" is a contested term and we are not interested here in striking a definitive definition. Nor are we interested in a theoretical model applicable to all parts of the world. Rather, we are interested in identifying democratic benchmarks relevant to Canada in the twenty-first century. In selecting these we were guided by the issues raised in the current literature on Canadian democratic practice and by the concerns commonly raised by opinion leaders and found in public opinion data. We have settled on three benchmarks: public participation, inclusiveness, and responsiveness. We believe that any contemporary definition of Canadian democracy must include institutions and decision-making practices that are defined by public participation, that this participation must include all Canadians, and that government outcomes must respond to the views of Canadians.

While settling on these guiding principles, we have not imposed a strict set of democratic criteria on all of the evaluations that together constitute the Audit. Rather, our approach allows the auditors wide latitude in their evaluations. While all auditors keep the benchmarks of participation, inclusiveness, and responsiveness central to their examinations, each adds additional criteria of particular importance to the subject he or she is considering. We believe this approach of identifying unifying themes, while allowing for divergent perspectives, enhances the project by capturing the robustness of the debate surrounding democratic norms and practices.

We decided at the outset to cover substantial ground and to do so in a relatively short period. These two considerations, coupled with a desire to respond to the most commonly raised criticisms of the contemporary practice of Canadian democracy, result in a series that focuses on public institutions, electoral practices, and new phenomena that are likely to affect democratic life significantly. The series includes volumes that examine key public decision-making bodies: legislatures, the courts, and cabinets and government. The structures of our democratic system are considered in volumes devoted to questions of federalism and the electoral system. The ways in which citizens participate in electoral politics and policy making are a crucial component of the project, and thus we include studies of advocacy groups and political

parties. The desire and capacity of Canadians for meaningful participation in public life is the subject of a volume. Finally, the challenges
and opportunities raised by new communication technologies are also
considered. The Audit does not include studies devoted to the status of
particular groups of Canadians. Rather than separate out Aboriginals,
women, new Canadians, and others, these groups are treated together
with all Canadians throughout the Audit.

In all, this series includes nine volumes examining specific areas of
Canadian democratic life. A tenth, synthetic volume provides an overall assessment and makes sense out of the different approaches and
findings found in the rest of the series. Our examination is not exhaustive. Canadian democracy is a vibrant force, the status of which can
never be fully captured at one time. Nonetheless the areas we consider
involve many of the pressing issues currently facing democracy in
Canada. We do not expect to have the final word on this subject. Rather,
we hope to encourage others to pursue similar avenues of inquiry.

A project of this scope cannot be accomplished without the support
of many individuals. At the top of the list of those deserving credit are
the members of the Canadian Democratic Audit team. From the very
beginning, the Audit has been a team effort. This outstanding group of
academics has spent many hours together, defining the scope of the
project, prodding each other on questions of Canadian democracy, and
most important, supporting one another throughout the endeavour,
all with good humour. To Darin Barney, André Blais, Kenneth Carty,
John Courtney, David Docherty, Joanna Everitt, Elisabeth Gidengil, Ian
Greene, Richard Nadeau, Neil Nevitte, Richard Sigurdson, Jennifer
Smith, Frank Strain, Michael Tucker, Graham White, and Lisa Young I
am forever grateful.

The Centre for Canadian Studies at Mount Allison University has
been my intellectual home for several years. The Centre, along with the
Harold Crabtree Foundation, has provided the necessary funding and
other assistance necessary to see this project through to fruition. At
Mount Allison University, Peter Ennals provided important support to
this project when others were skeptical; Wayne MacKay and Michael Fox
have continued this support since their respective arrivals on campus;

and Joanne Goodrich and Peter Loewen have provided important technical and administrative help.

The University of British Columbia Press, particularly its senior acquisitions editor, Emily Andrew, has been a partner in this project from the very beginning. Emily has been involved in every important decision and has done much to improve the result. Camilla Blakeley has overseen the copyediting and production process and in doing so has made these books better. Scores of Canadian and international political scientists have participated in the project as commentators at our public conferences, as critics at our private meetings, as providers of quiet advice, and as referees of the volumes. The list is too long to name them all, but David Cameron, Sid Noel, Leslie Seidle, Jim Bickerton, Alexandra Dobrowolsky, Livianna Tossutti, Janice Gross Stein, and Frances Abele all deserve special recognition for their contributions. We are also grateful to the Canadian Study of Parliament Group, which partnered with us for our inaugural conference in Ottawa in November 2001.

Finally, this series is dedicated to all of the men and women who contribute to the practice of Canadian democracy. Whether as active participants in parties, groups, courts, or legislatures, or in the media and the universities, without them Canadian democracy would not survive.

William Cross
Director, The Canadian Democratic Audit

INTRODUCTION

This book presents an audit of the current state of Canada's courts as the third branch of our democracy. This is not an audit in the sense of a financial audit of a corporation by a chartered accounting firm, or an accountability audit of a government department by the auditor general. Rather, it is an attempt to evaluate the adequacy of the Canadian court system in relation to the basic tenets of democracy.

But what, you may well ask, do the courts have to do with democracy? Our judges are appointed rather than elected, and they are drawn from an elite group in society. The judges are not accountable for their decisions, and yet from time to time they seem to meddle with the policies of elected governments. Some might even argue that the courts function as a bulwark against democracy. In fact, some prominent academics both on the right and the left are deeply troubled by what they consider to be the increasingly antidemocratic role assumed by our courts, especially since the Charter of Rights and Freedoms came into effect in 1982.

Democracy requires an independent judiciary. Our political system can function fairly only with courts staffed by judges who are not accountable for their decisions – not accountable so that they can be independent and impartial. Only judges who are in a position to be independent and impartial can settle disputes justly about the application and interpretation of laws enacted by elected legislatures, even in cases when interpretation overlaps with policy making. This audit of the performance of courts in Canada's democracy is conducted in the context of this paradox.

When thinking about the courts and democracy, the debate about judicial policy making can become so absorbing that other important aspects of the link between courts and democracy may be overlooked. The judicial policy-making issue aside, courts in a democracy need to provide a fair, expeditious, and effective dispute-resolution service that is as open as practically possible to public participation and the inclusion of all relevant groups. Courts also need to be responsive to legitimate public needs and demands. These aspects of the relationship between courts and democracy are front and centre in this audit, and the judicial policy-making issue will be treated as just one element of the link, albeit an important one. There is therefore less concern in the pages that follow about judicial activism than "Charterphobes" would prefer (Sigurdson 1993), and more attention is paid to whether judicial decisions are likely to promote democratic principles.

Canadian courts provide a publicly funded and sponsored adjudication service for settling legal disputes. A system of courts is an essential part of any democratic regime, and without courts no democracy could function. This audit will provide one person's assessment of the extent to which the courts are achieving their essential purpose: to resolve the kinds of disputes that elected legislatures have given them responsibility for in a fair, effective, and efficient manner and according to standards derived from democratic norms. Three benchmarks of democracy guide the analysis presented here: participation, inclusiveness, and responsiveness. The Canadian Democratic Audit has chosen these three standards as tools to help assess the current state of Canadian democracy with respect to several key institutions and processes including legislatures, cabinets, elections, parties, and interest groups, in addition to the courts.

We live in a representative democracy. But there is the ever-present danger that representative assemblies, if disproportionately made up by the socially or economically powerful, can become elitist, thus discouraging optimal public participation. Another peril is that some representatives will inevitably be more focused on self-interest than the public interest (Stein 2002). These inherent weaknesses of representative democracy might be compounded by courts. Courts that serve democracy faithfully, however, will act as a counterweight to the tendency toward the elitist and self-interested exercise of power by members of the legislative and executive branches.

Ironically, the courts themselves have always been an elite institution. Because of the expertise required of judges, the judiciary will always be recruited from the lawyers who have demonstrated the highest levels of success in law school and their legal careers. But there are legitimate ways to promote the recruitment of judges from groups that have tended not to enjoy a privileged position in society. The independence that we provide to judges by insulating them from political pressures and providing them with salaries so high that financial gain ought to be of no concern, moreover, means that judges ought to be in a position to decide issues based on the public interest, and not self-interest.

Courts had their origins centuries before the democratic era. When democratic institutions began to be introduced into what is now Canada, the courts were not the object of democratic reforms, and they still retain many of their predemocratic trappings. Democracy was introduced with the establishment of elected legislatures in the colonies, and democratic reforms continued with the acceptance of responsible government, and with the expansion of the franchise to include men without property, then women, then Asian Canadians, and then Aboriginal Canadians. The "rights revolution" (Ignatieff 2000) of the latter half of the twentieth century and the concurrent development of more stringent rules to promote higher ethical standards among elected politicians (Greene and Shugarman 1997), along with the interest of some academics and politicians in the promotion of greater public participation in policy making (Albo, Langille, and Panitch 1993), are all examples of the continued evolution of Canadian democracy.

Until recently, the courts remained unaffected by most of the democratic reforms going on around them. Until judicial selection procedures changed in the late twentieth century (Chapter 1), judicial appointment was based primarily on party patronage considerations. As well, the courts tended to be administered as semi-independent fiefdoms, under the general direction of judges, or politically appointed court officials, or Crown attorneys, depending on who had the strongest personality in a given court district. There was precious little supervision from head office officials and almost no consultation with nonlawyer court "users" - litigants, witnesses, and jurors - about administrative issues that affected them (Greene 1983). The situation has improved a little during the past two decades but the public still has very little opportunity to participate, directly or indirectly, in the administration of courts.

Given that the courts clearly are not leading examples of democratically run organizations, it is nevertheless true that the courts have come to be used as vehicles to promote progressive policy changes by groups claiming to promote democratic reform. In fact, public interest litigation was unusual before the 1970s. One of the first such cases developed in 1927, when five women who were leading proponents of women's equality spearheaded litigation that eventually led to a decision by the Judicial Committee of the Privy Council (at that time the ultimate court of appeal for Canada) that henceforth women were to be considered as legal "persons," and therefore eligible for appointment to the Senate (*Edwards* v. *Canada (A.G.)* 1930). Aside from rare cases like this one, there was relatively little public interest litigation until the 1960s, when groups began to form to further human rights by taking cases to court under the 1960 Canadian Bill of Rights and nascent provincial human rights legislation. The Canadian Civil Liberties Association (CCLA), now one of the most active public interest litigators, was formed in 1964 by people concerned about the potential abuse of police powers in Ontario. The federal Court Challenges Program, dating from 1977, has encouraged public interest groups to use the courts to pursue their language rights, and after the advent of the Charter, groups such as the Women's Legal Education and Action Fund (LEAF) have sought broader equality rights through the courts.

The Approach of the Book

This book provides an "insider's perspective" on Canada's courts. I have been fortunate during my academic career to have conducted formal interviews with about a hundred judges at all levels of court, as well as with dozens of trial lawyers, Crown attorneys, administrative staff in the courts, litigants, and witnesses. As well, I have had countless informal discussions with members of these groups. In 1979 and 1980, as part of my doctoral research, I conducted interviews in Ontario with a representative sample of forty judges at all levels, and with at least thirty people from each of the following groups: trial lawyers, court administrators, and Crown attorneys. The research centred on the causes of unreasonable delays in the courts (Greene 1983). During the early 1980s, Peter McCormick and I interviewed members of these same groups in Alberta (using a sample about the same size as the Ontario study) as part of a research project that focused on the judicial decision-making process (McCormick and Greene 1990). We also interviewed witnesses and litigants to gain a sense of their satisfaction with the courts. During the early 1990s, I interviewed more than fifty appeal court judges from across Canada, including eight judges of the Supreme Court of Canada, and colleagues of mine interviewed another fifty appellate court judges. The purpose of that study was to compare administrative and decision-making processes among the ten provincial appeal courts, the Federal Court (Appeal Division), and the Supreme Court of Canada (Greene et al. 1998).

In addition to spending much of my career studying courts, I have also participated in litigation. I have served as an expert witness in four cases (three dealing with judicial independence, and one concerning the refugee determination process). In two of these, I was subjected to intense cross-examination. What I learned from these experiences is that it is one thing to defend social science research findings in academic journals and books, and quite another to defend these findings in court. In some senses, the standard of proof is higher, but in other senses, so much depends on strategies of counsel and the discretion of the judges that the search for truth sometimes gets lost in the legal exercise. And like many Canadians, in my younger years I once went to court to fight what I thought was an unfair traffic ticket. The justice of the peace was aghast at my elaborately prepared defence and dismissed the case because he didn't have time to hear it.

What I offer in this book is my own perspective, based on these experiences, on the state of Canada's courts. This perspective is both enlightened and limited by my personal adventures in the courts. These have taught me that administrative issues are as important to evaluating the democratic impact of courts as judicial decisions that impact major policy issues. The question of judicial activism, which is central to the analysis of Canada's courts by many contemporary academics and politicians, is clearly salient, but it is neither the only issue nor even the most important one. What is central is the extent to which the courts and those who populate them - including the judges but not forgetting court staff, lawyers, prosecutors, litigants, and witnesses - reflect three key indicators of democracy: participation, inclusiveness, and responsiveness.

The Plan of the Book

In order to understand the nature of the entity being audited, Chapter 1 provides an overview of the Canadian court system and some of the current debates about the courts and democracy. Chapter 2 reviews the nature of, and opportunities for, public participation in Canada's courts. Chapter 3 deals with inclusiveness issues, such as the extent to which the major actors in the courts - judges, lawyers, court staff, and litigants - are representative of Canadian society. Chapters 4 and 5 address the responsiveness benchmark. The focus of Chapter 4 is on the courts' sensitivity to public demands for a fair and effective dispute-resolution service, while Chapter 5 assesses the impact of public interest litigation, especially under the Charter of Rights. The final chapter provides my own recommendations for improvements that, I hope, will result in a court system that can more effectively serve Canadian democracy.

Democracy is an ideal toward which our society has been evolving for centuries. The democratic ideal is based on the principle of mutual respect, that is, recognition of the intrinsic worth of every human being. From this principle, it logically follows that a democracy must include safeguards for individual dignity and equality, legislatures composed of accountable representatives selected through free and fair elections with limited terms, active public participation in the development of public policy, and the rule of law enforced by independent and impartial courts (Greene and Shugarman 1997). These principles can be summed up in the three touchstones of the Canadian Democratic Audit: participation, inclusiveness, and responsiveness. True democracy will never be fully realized because of human frailties, but it is a goal worth striving for because of its emphasis on the equal dignity of every human being.

The courts, as the state's officially sanctioned institutions for dispute resolution, existed for centuries before democratic times, and thus they have inherited a tendency to be hierarchical and elitist. Peter Russell (1975, 88), the father of the political science study of the law, has noted that "for too many lawyers and judges, judging is still not regarded as the provision of a basic social service but the exercise of a private professional craft." To what extent have we built a court system that truly serves democracy, and what are some of the goals that the courts might aim for during this new century in order to serve democracy better? These are the basic questions tackled in the pages that follow.

THE COURTS

CANADA'S COURTS IN CONTEXT 1

In order to evaluate courts, we need to understand their purpose and objectives. Although courts – the institutions where judges practice their trade – have a history rooted in predemocratic traditions, the advent of democracy has changed the nature of, and public expectations for, courts. This chapter describes the history, role, and constitutional context of the Canadian court system.

The Function of Courts in Historical Context

In complex societies, three features are common to governments: leaders, laws, and judges. Once a society reaches a certain degree of complexity, it needs an institutional means for resolving the kinds of disputes that might otherwise threaten the stability of the social order. For example, Canadian Aboriginal societies prior to European contact had sophisticated dispute-resolution procedures based on the authority of elders and consensual decision making by male or female councils (Boldt, Long, and Little Bear 1985). And references in the Old Testament to the administration of justice indicate that at the time of Moses, rulers were preoccupied with issues of adjudication similar to those of today: the quest for fairness in settling disputes under the law, and the question of how to eliminate unacceptable backlogs of cases (Exodus 18:13-27).

As Rome expanded beginning in the third century BC, formal legal actions could be initiated before patrician priests – the earliest Roman judges. Then as now, many legal proceedings resulted from disagreements over business and property interests. Because commerce requires a stable and predictable system of enforceable rules, the judge-made law that had developed was eventually codified to clarify it. After the fall of the Roman Empire, these codes were gradually incorporated into the laws of many European countries over the next four centuries. In England of the thirteenth to eighteenth centuries, however, there was skepticism about codifying judge-made law, possibly because judges had assumed a very high status in society, drawn as they were from the ranks of senior lawyers. Therefore English "common law," or judge-made law common to the whole land, remained an important ingredient of the law, in contrast to the "civil law" tradition on the Continent, where judicial precedent played a less central role. Quebec has inherited the French civil law approach with regard to its private law system, but is a common law jurisdiction regarding public law (constitutional, administrative, and criminal law). The other provinces are situated entirely within the common law realm (Gall 2004). Thus, Canada has inherited both of the great European legal traditions.

The structure of Canadian courts is rooted in the English court system. After the Norman conquest in 1066, disputes about the application of the king's law in Norman England were settled by the king himself to begin with, or by king and council. The central royal courts and the circuit courts (with names such as King's Bench and Common Pleas) were established beginning in the twelfth century as a response to the ever-increasing caseload (Holdsworth 1903). These central and circuit courts created by the monarch became known as "superior" courts, while local courts were referred to as "inferior" courts. The Canadian superior courts (such as the Alberta Court of Queen's Bench and the Ontario Superior Court) and inferior courts (such as the Provincial Court of British Columbia and the Court of Quebec) are the descendants of these early English institutions.

In Norman times the superior court judges were clerics, but allegations of bribery, followed by a royal commission inquiry, led to the firing of many of them in the late thirteenth century. To fill the vacated judicial seats, the king began to appoint men from the newly developing legal profession. By the middle of the fourteenth century, it had become the established tradition for the English king to select the superior court judges from the ranks of experienced lawyers (Dawson 1968). This system of judicial recruitment contrasted with the approach on the European continent, where separate training schools for judges were established. The most successful graduates were appointed to the minor courts, and the ablest were eventually promoted to higher judicial offices (Abraham 1998). Canada has inherited the English method of judicial recruitment.

The year 1688 is central to the evolution of courts in democracies with the British parliamentary system. In that year in England and Wales, the Glorious Revolution ended the absolute power of the monarchy and created a constitutional, or limited, monarchy. One important element of the new regime was the recognition of Parliament as the supreme law-making body. Another change was the recognition of the rule of law: citizens were subject only to laws approved by Parliament, and not to arbitrary decrees of powerful members of the executive or public service. The rule of law also required "indifferent" judges to settle disputes under the law, something that could happen only if judges were independent (Locke [1690] 1980). After the Glorious Revolution, it was accepted that the superior courts had to be independent in their decision-making capacity, free from interference either from the executive and the public service, or from Parliament.

The resolution of serious disputes according to law as expeditiously and impartially as possible is the central purpose of courts in a democracy. The courts, however, cannot avoid a law-clarification function in some cases, and this role is often referred to as the "law-making" or "policy-making" role of courts. The law is composed of words, and many words and phrases are open to two or more equally legitimate interpretations. Judges must use their discretion to choose the interpretation that to them appears to be the most just. In a democratic context, it is naturally expected that judicial discretion will be exercised in accordance with democratic values. Thus, one secondary purpose of courts is to create rules to fill in the gaps left by legislation.

Does the law-making function of the courts, in the sense described above, contradict the principle of the rule of law by elected legislatures, and thus compromise democracy? The position taken here is that there is no reason judicial discretion must necessarily undermine democracy. Rather, the appropriate use of judicial discretion might actually strengthen democracy. It all depends on the context surrounding the use of discretion, and the impact of discretionary decisions, as will be demonstrated in the examples in Chapter 5. Martin Shapiro (1981) has shown that one common result of the use of judicial discretion is the enforcement of prevailing social norms. Some of these judicially enforced norms are the result of a popular consensus; others may represent elite values displaced onto more vulnerable parts of the population. The former application of judicial discretion is more democratic than the latter.

With the evolution of democracy, the judicial branch of government has become an institution that serves as a check on the legislative and executive branches of government. Representative legislatures, and the cabinets that control them, are always in danger of abrogating the liberal democratic principles of equality and freedom. This danger stems from the temptation of those with political power to act in self-interest rather than the public interest, from the tendency of majorities to overlook the legitimate equality rights of minorities that they have little in common with, and from the fact that a great deal of legislation is enacted on the recommendation of professional bureaucrats who have their own particular needs and interests. Another secondary purpose of courts, therefore, is to function as part of a system of checks and balances designed to prevent abuses of power.

In sum, representative democracy requires a complex set of compensating mechanisms to prevent abuse of power and to ensure fairness, and the judiciary is intended to play a key role in helping to ensure that these rules are applied fairly and effectively – even to the judiciary itself.

The Canadian Court System

There are two basic kinds of courts: trial and appellate. The trial courts are the courts of first instance, where judges settle the criminal, civil, constitutional, or administrative law disputes brought to them that they have jurisdiction over. Trial courts constitute the basic workhorse of the court system, and they often specialize in settling either criminal law or private law matters. In most cases, a litigant who disagrees with the trial judge's decision can appeal it. Every province in Canada has a Court of Appeal established as an institution separate from the trial courts, and these courts hear the most difficult appeals. As well, the Federal Court, the court that hears federal administrative law cases, has an Appeal Division. Appeals from trial courts in Yukon are heard by the British Columbia Court of Appeal, and from the trial courts in the Northwest Territories and Nunavut by the Alberta Court of Appeal. (Appeals from very minor cases are sometimes heard by judges in higher trial courts.) Very rarely, cases are appealed from the provincial courts of appeal or the Federal Court (Appeal Division) to the Supreme Court of Canada. Litigants unhappy with the outcome of an appeal from a provincial court of appeal of the Federal Court (Appeal Division) can apply to the Supreme Court for permission to appeal, and every year there are about 600 of these applications. The Supreme Court hears only cases that it considers of national legal importance, however, and these amount to about eighty annually. As well, there is a right of appeal to the Supreme Court in serious criminal cases where the trial and appeal courts have rendered different decisions, or where there has been a dissenting judgment in the provincial court of appeal, and there are a few dozen of these annually.

In the Canadian system, trial judges always sit alone, except in the relatively infrequent cases in which they are assisted by a jury. This contrasts with Europe and many other parts of the world, where trial judges in criminal cases often sit in panels of three, or preside along with two lay (non-judge) assessors. Judges in the separate Courts of Appeal almost always hear appeals in panels. The provincial and federal appellate courts usually sit in panels of three but occasionally in panels of five for cases raising high profile issues of law. The Supreme Court of Canada, with its nine judges, often sits in panels of seven, although sometimes in panels of five or nine, depending on the chief justice's allocation of judicial resources.

In Canada, the authority for the administration of adjudicative matters is split between the federal and provincial governments, but it is not split along the lines of their division of powers, as in the United States. The fathers of the Canadian Confederation had observed the difficulties encountered by Americans as a result of their separate system of courts for cases arising out of federal laws, which operated parallel to the state and municipal courts. Canada opted for a court system that would be primarily unitary, capable of settling disputes arising out of federal, provincial, and municipal laws. Therefore, the 1867 Constitution allocated specific responsibilities for maintaining the primarily unitary court system to each order of government. Although this is an ingenious approach to the need for a relatively simple court structure in a federal system, it means that federal-provincial cooperation is needed to resolve many administrative issues in the courts, and that cooperation is not always there.

The federal government was assigned responsibility for the appointment of superior court judges (provincial superior court trial judges with jurisdiction similar to the superior courts in the UK) and provincial appellate judges. The superior court judges travel around their province or provincial region holding hearings or "assizes" like the English judges of old, visiting smaller centres twice a year. The provinces retained control over the appointment of all inferior judges, such as the judges of the magistrate's courts, which generally became known as Provincial Courts beginning in the late 1960s. Parliament was also given power to establish a Supreme Court of Canada – which it did in 1875 – and other courts to adjudicate disputes arising out of a limited set of federal laws. There are two of these latter courts: the Federal Court, established in 1971 as a continuance of the Exchequer Court of 1875, and the Tax Court, set up in 1983.

In 2004, there were 2,038 judges in Canada, including 240 supernumerary (partly retired) judges. Fifty-two percent of the judges were federal judicial appointments, and the remainder were appointed by the provinces or territories. During the fiscal year 2000-1, the total expenditure on judicial salaries at all levels was $382,170,000, or $12.42 per capita, which is about two-fifths of the total expenditure on court operations (Snowball 2002). In 2004, superior court trial and appellate judges earned $221,400 annually, while Supreme Court judges and the chief justices in all the superior courts earned somewhat more.

The Constitution gave the federal government the responsibility for the criminal law, while the provinces retained control over most private law matters. The provinces kept their pre-Confederation responsibility for prosecuting criminal offences in all courts, and also for providing court facilities and staff for all courts in the unitary system below the level of the Supreme Court. In the late 1960s, however, the federal government assumed responsibility for the prosecution of federal offences that are not part of the criminal law (such as drug offences). The only courts that are exceptions to the unitary court system are the Federal Court and Federal Court of Appeal, whose forty-seven judges hear cases dealing primarily with federal administrative law issues, and the Tax Court, whose twenty-seven judges hear cases arising out of federal taxation laws (see Figure 1.1). The division of powers over the justice system is set out in sections 96 to 101, 91(27), and 92(14 and 15) of the Constitution Act, 1867.

Very serious criminal offences, such as murder, aggravated sexual assault, and armed robbery are referred to as "indictable" offences. The Canadian Criminal Code stipulates that these cases must be heard by a superior court judge, and the Charter of Rights guarantees that in any case where an accused person is liable to receive a prison sentence of five years or more if convicted, the accused has a right to a trial by jury. Minor offences, such as shoplifting or petty theft, are known as "summary conviction" offences, and are tried by a provincially appointed judge. A great many offences in the Criminal Code are known as "hybrid" offences, less serious than the purely indictable offences, but more serious than the purely summary conviction offences. This means that the Crown attorney prosecuting the offence may opt to proceed by way of indictment, meaning that the possible penalty is

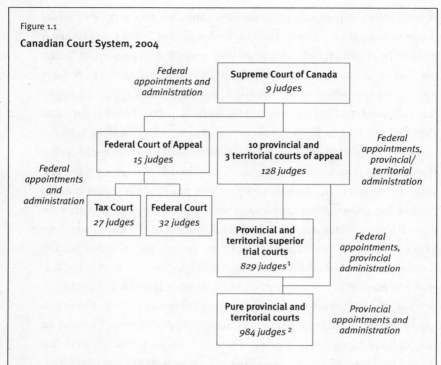

Figure 1.1

Canadian Court System, 2004

Federal appointments and administration

Supreme Court of Canada
9 judges

Federal Court of Appeal
15 judges

10 provincial and 3 territorial courts of appeal
128 judges

Federal appointments, provincial/ territorial administration

Federal appointments and administration

Tax Court
27 judges

Federal Court
32 judges

Provincial and territorial superior trial courts
829 judges[1]

Federal appointments, provincial administration

Pure provincial and territorial courts
984 judges [2]

Provincial appointments and administration

Notes: In 2003, the Federal Court (Appeal Division) became a separate court – the Federal Court of Appeal. With the Tax Court, these three courts are now known collectively as the federal courts. Numbers in the diagram include supernumerary, or partly retired, judges but not vacancies. There were 193 supernumerary judges in the provincial superior courts, four each on the Federal Court of Appeal and Federal Court, and five on the Tax Court. There were twelve vacancies on the provincial superior trial courts, three on the provincial appellate courts, five on the Federal Court, and two on the Federal Court of Appeal. Family judges on the Superior Courts are included.

1   In addition, there are 22 traditional and case management masters in Ontario and 54 masters in British Columbia.

2   In addition, there are 274 justices of the peace, 134 Municipal Court judges in Ontario, and 104 Municipal Court judges in Quebec. Other provinces also employ justices of the peace.

Source: Snowball (2002), updated by the author from data supplied by the Office of the Commissioner for Federal Judicial Affairs, Ottawa, and the *Canada Law List* (2004).

potentially more severe, or by way of summary conviction, meaning that the possible penalty will be less severe. In cases where the Crown has opted to proceed by way of indictment, or where the Criminal Code defines an offence as indictable, the accused often has the right to opt for a trial by jury in a superior court, or a trial by judge alone in a superior court or a court with a provincially appointed judge (sometimes the consent of the Crown is required), depending on the nature of the offence.

In civil cases, a defendant may opt for a jury trial in cases where the plaintiff is suing for substantial amounts, except in cases involving libel, slander, seduction, malicious arrest or prosecution, or false imprisonment. Even in these cases, however, the jury can be waived with the agreement of both sides. Jury trials are now very uncommon in civil cases: less than 6 percent of civil trials involve juries. And in the criminal field, less than 2 percent of cases involving indictable offences (and none involving summary conviction offences) end in jury trials (Russell 1987).

It is worthwhile visiting the courts at different levels to compare their general atmospheres. Most of the cases heard in the superior courts are civil or private law cases, and so most litigants are relatively well-to-do, including many corporate litigants. Most of the cases heard in the inferior courts relate to criminal or provincial offences, and most litigants appear to be at the lower end of the socio-economic status scale. Superior court proceedings, whether criminal or civil, tend to be conducted with solemnity and dignity, while the inferior courts are more frequently overcrowded and unpleasant.

It should be noted that most civil and criminal cases are settled without going to a full adversary trial. Settlement occurs either because the judge's decision in a particular case is so predictable that there is no sense wasting time in a trial, or because the decision is so unpredictable due to discretionary factors that a settlement between the parties in advance of a trial eliminates uncertainty. On the civil side, more than 95 percent of cases filed do not go to trial, but are settled out of court or abandoned by the plaintiff. On the criminal side, more than 90 percent of cases are settled as a result of a simple guilty plea, or a plea bargain that results in a guilty plea (Greene et al. 1998, 44).

In order for the adjudicative process to be credible and to serve the needs of democracy, several conditions have to be met. Judges must be competent and must attempt to decide as impartially as possible. They also need to appear to be in a position to be impartial. In cases involving jury trials, the selected jurors should be impartial and competent, and they should be treated with respect. Litigants must be treated fairly, meaning that due process is followed so that both sides in a dispute have the opportunity to present their cases fully. Finally, cases must be settled in a timely fashion. In criminal cases, this means that after taking into account the reasonable time needed by criminal accused persons or their lawyers and the Crown to prepare their cases, cases ought to be tried with minimal delay. Accused persons should not have to suffer long waits during which their fate is uncertain, and during which time they might be incarcerated. As well, the longer the delay, the less reliable is the memory of witnesses, and the less chance there is that witnesses will still be available to testify. In civil cases, unnecessary delays not only lead to suffering because of unknown outcomes, but where large sums of money are involved, delays in paying settlements can lead to additional injustices.

Judicial Impartiality, Appointment, and Education

Perfect impartiality, for judges or for anyone else, is impossible. The impossibility of total impartiality is no reason to become cynical about the quest for justice, however, just as the fact that no professor is perfectly impartial is not a good enough reason to give up on examinations and graded essays as a teaching tool. What we expect of judges is for them to be educated, selected, and situated so as to be as impartial as humanly possible in the context of democratic values.

Judicial education in Canada consists of completing a law degree, and having at least ten years of experience in legal practice or as a law school professor. Until thirty years ago, there were no formal training courses for judges; life experience and experience in legal practice were considered sufficient. In 1971 the Canadian Judicial Council was established with both an education and a discipline mandate for federally appointed judges. It sponsored several educational seminars for judges each year, including one in judgment writing. From 1974, the Canadian Institute for the Administration of Justice has run educational seminars for judges at all levels, including a one-week seminar for new judges. In 1987 the National Judicial Institute was established in Ottawa to develop and deliver educational programs for judges at all levels and across Canada. Judicial attendance at these educational seminars is not required, and depends on the interest of individual judges, availability of a budget to cover costs, and the willingness of chief judges and justices to allow puisne (ordinary) judges to attend.

Interviews with superior court judges conducted in the mid-1990s revealed that most judges thought that they did not have adequate time for judicial education (Greene et al. 1998). Given that the European civil law tradition has created compulsory academic training programs for aspiring judges that are separate from the training programs for lawyers, and given the spate of wrongful convictions brought to light by DNA testing (Manitoba 2001), it is natural to wonder whether the Canadian system for judicial training could be improved. As well, judges would probably be more effective in contributing to solutions to the administrative problems in courts if they had some training in courts administration. For example, newly appointed judges might be required to attend a comprehensive judicial training program of several months' duration before taking up their positions, or universities could provide postgraduate programs in adjudication for aspiring judges or tribunal members. Some of the training programs currently offered by the National Judicial Institute deal with strategies for reducing bias related to such factors as gender. In order to promote impartial decision making, it would be useful to ensure that such strategies are known and available for use by all judges, not just those who choose to and are able to take such courses. Whatever enhancements are made to judicial training must necessarily be set up so as to avoid interference with judicial independence. Once they've taken up their positions, that is, judges cannot be required to take specific courses, as this mechanism might be used to tamper with judicial independence.

The procedures for making judicial appointments in Canada have improved greatly during the past three decades. Up to the 1960s, political patronage was a major factor in judicial appointments at both the federal and provincial levels. The first cracks in the patronage system began to appear in 1967, when Pierre Trudeau was minister of justice. He set up a system of consultation in which a committee of the Canadian Bar Association reviewed candidates for federal judicial appointments being considered by the office of the minister of justice, and rated them as to whether they were "qualified" for a judicial appointment. As well, the recruitment of candidates for federal judicial appointments became more systematic when an official in the minister's office was designated to prescreen candidates who had expressed interest in a judicial position, and to look for additional names to put on the list through an informal system of contacts. The cabinet rarely appointed anyone deemed "unqualified" by the Bar Association screening committee. Patronage still played an important role, however, because those who got on the list in the first place were those acceptable to the justice minister and the prime minister.

In 1968 Ontario's Royal Commission into Civil Rights, led by former chief justice James McRuer, pointed out the problems of bias and unfairness created by magistrates appointed by the provincial cabinet for their political connections rather than their competence (McRuer 1968). As a result of McRuer's scathing critique of the provincial justice system, the magistrate's courts were replaced by a provincial court with better facilities and higher qualifications for judges. Judicial appointments were screened by a judicial council, which, like the Trudeau system at the federal level, at least weeded out potentially bad appointments. The other provinces followed suit with revised judicial appointments systems, and for a while they seemed to compete to develop the best system for making quality appointments. Patronage as a factor in judicial appointments nearly disappeared completely in some of the Western provinces, although it remained an important factor in some of the Atlantic provinces (Canadian Bar Association 1985).

Extensive reforms were made to the Ontario provincial judges appointment system in the late 1980s by Attorney General Ian Scott. The thirteen-member committee that eventually resulted from Scott's reforms was initially chaired by one of Canada's leading academic authorities on the judiciary, Peter Russell (1992). The appointments committee is composed of a nearly equal number of lawyers and nonlawyers, and of men and women. The key feature of this committee is that it actively recruits potential candidates, rather than simply reacting to names provided by the government. It advertises extensively for qualified persons to apply for judicial positions and has been particularly proactive in encouraging women and members of minority groups to apply. Applicants must complete a comprehensive application form, and references are checked. Those who appear to be best qualified are interviewed and ranked. The committee forwards its ranked recommendations to the Ontario Judicial Council, which forwards them to the attorney general. Until the Conservative government under Mike Harris took office in 1995, the cabinet nearly always appointed the candidates recommended by the committee. For a time, the Conservative attorney general was of the opinion that the appointments committee tended to recommend candidates who were not tough enough on crime, and asked the committee for a longer list of potential appointees. Eventually, however, the Harris cabinet was persuaded by supporters of the new system that the judicial appointments committee system was fair after all, and resulted in higher-quality appointments than had previously been the case. All the other provinces and territories have judicial appointments advisory committees of some sort (see Chapter 2).

The improvements at the provincial level encouraged the federal government to enhance the system for federal judicial appointments. The Mulroney government replaced the system of consultation with the Canadian Bar Association with provincially based screening committees, and the responsibility for creating the list of potential candidates was transferred from the justice minister's office to the commissioner for federal judicial affairs. This new system, however, represented only a small improvement. The committees were not given responsibility for recruiting candidates. All they could do was to attempt to screen out unqualified candidates presented by the commissioner – a very limited function. The Liberal election platform of 1993 included a promise to improve this system, and there have in fact been some enhancements since then, using the Ontario system as a model. The committees advertise to encourage a broader range of applicants, applicants must fill out application forms similar to those used in Ontario, and the committees may interview applicants. But although the federal government has promised since 1993 to make public the names of committee members, this has still not occurred, and attempts to encourage qualified applicants to apply for a federal judgeship are still not as extensive as the Ontario procedures.

There is no committee system in place to assist with the recruitment of candidates for the Supreme Court of Canada, or for elevations from trial courts to appellate courts. Decisions about appointments to the Supreme Court have always been made by the prime minister in consultation with the minister of justice, taking into account the need for a balanced representation of regions, and background factors such as religion and ethnicity. (By law, three of the nine judges must be appointed from Quebec.) Beginning in the Trudeau period, attempts were made to take political partisanship out of the appointment process, and to appoint persons to the Supreme Court who were generally considered to be the best potential judges in the country – still taking into account, of course, factors such as regional representation and, after 1982, the approach the candidate might take to the interpretation of the Charter. Very little is known about how decisions are made by the federal cabinet to elevate trial court judges to provincial appellate courts. Decisions about the chief justiceships of the superior courts are made by the prime minister, and the chief judges of the provincial courts have traditionally been appointed by the premier and the attorney general, although in some provinces the regular judges now have a role in selecting the chief judge.

The Democratic Role of Courts

Courts are the state's officially sanctioned institutions for conflict resolution. Their primary purpose is the authoritative resolution of disputes that elected legislatures have determined should come within their purview. They also have secondary purposes: to create rules that fill in the gaps left by legislation, to protect the principles of limited government stemming from equality and freedom, and to enforce the rules designed to prevent the opportunities for abuse of power inherent in representative democracy. Even where statute law is as clear as possible, it is rarely completely unambiguous, and so the exercise of judicial discretion is unavoidable. In a democracy, judges are expected to use this discretion in accord with democratic values.

When Canada was established in 1867, this country was on the road to democracy because of the Constitution's provision for a representative Parliament and provincial legislatures, and the tradition of responsible government that promoted cabinet accountability to the elected legislature. After the franchise became universal in the first half of the twentieth century, some of the vestiges of the predemocratic era of courts – patronage appointments, and a system built to allow lawyers and judges more to practise their craft than to serve the public – began to give way to merit-based systems of appointment and reorganized court services that placed greater emphasis on service to the public.

After the Charter of Rights came into being in 1982, many Canadians began to realize what has always been the case – that courts have an unavoidable policy-making role whenever the law is unclear. Some laws, such as constitutions, are at high levels of abstraction, and therefore are unavoidably vague. Although some academics and politicians have been critical of the activism of Canadian courts since 1982, and although most Canadians think that their courts need to be more sensitive and compassionate, most of us are considerably more trusting of the courts than of elected legislatures. (This is not to imply that this imbalance is acceptable; clearly, reforms are needed that will generate a significantly higher level of trust in elected legislatures.) The controversy over the law-making role of judges is based in part on the assumption that democracy is simply government by a majority of elected legislators. Thinking about democracy more broadly as government by consent, with consequent implications of equality, liberty, and representative government, leaves open the consideration of aspects of democracy to which the courts can and should contribute. Chapter 2 turns to the issue of public participation in the court system.

Chapter 1

Strengths

- Canada's court system is integrated, meaning that with just a few exceptions, cases arising out of both federal and provincial laws are tried in the same court system, and both the federal and provincial governments have important roles in administering and staffing the courts.

- Canada's court system builds on the strengths of the English common law system of courts and of adjudication, and incorporates some features of the French civil law system of adjudication in Quebec and in the federally established courts.

- Canada's judges have at least ten years' experience as lawyers before appointment to the courts.

Weaknesses

- Because both the federal and provincial governments have responsibilities for the court system, federal-provincial cooperation is required to ensure excellence in court administration, and that cooperation is not always evident.

- Canadian judges have very little specific training in adjudication or court administration.

- The hierarchy of courts results in lower-income Canadians forming the majority of litigants before the lower-income judges of the inferior courts, and higher-income Canadians and large corporations making up the majority of litigants before the higher-income judges of the superior courts.

PUBLIC PARTICIPATION IN THE JUSTICE SYSTEM

2

The judicial branch of government contrasts sharply with the executive and legislative branches because the rules governing court procedures severely restrict both the participation of the public and public accountability for judicial decisions. But these limitations also have benefits. In order to ensure that the will of the people, as expressed through the laws of elected legislatures, is put into effect and not manipulated by patronage and favouritism, the courts are insulated from all but the essential connections with the executive and legislative branches of government, and the public.

The downside of the insulation of the courts is that it can lead to a self-serving isolation if effective counterweights are not established – such as suitable accountability mechanisms (to be considered in Chapter 4), and appropriate input from the public during the adjudicative process.

The public can participate in court proceedings in several ways: through judicial selection procedures, observing court proceedings to prevent potential abuse, and court management committees. They can also participate as litigants, witnesses, jurors, intervenors, and expert witnesses. The following pages describe the contours of each of these potential avenues of participation and evaluate the extent to which they are utilized. How open are Canadian courts to public participation?

Public Participation in Judicial Selection

Historically, there has been precious little public participation in the selection of judges in Canada – not a sign of a vibrant democracy. Since 1867, federal or provincial cabinets have appointed judges at their own discretion, often out of patronage considerations. Beginning in the 1970s, as we saw in Chapter 1, judicial selection committees were created in a number of Canadian jurisdictions to provide more input into judicial selection from the legal profession and the public, with the expectation that this would result in better judges.

Since the 1960s, Peter Russell has drawn attention in his writings to the haphazard way in which Canadian judges are appointed. As a professor who specialized in the teaching of law and politics, he was dissatisfied with a system of judicial appointments based primarily on patronage. His concerns increased with the coming of the Charter of Rights, which from his perspective made it even more necessary than before to have an appointments system that resulted in the selection of the best possible judges (Russell 1987). Happily, when Ian Scott, Ontario's attorney general in the late 1980s, decided to reform the judicial appointments system for the province, he asked Russell to head the new Judicial Appointments Advisory Committee.

In 2004 lay members (people without a law degree) made up seven of the thirteen members of the Ontario Judicial Appointments Advisory Committee. Ontario is the only jurisdiction in Canada where lay members constitute the majority on a judicial recruitment or appointments screening committee. The committee also includes three judges appointed by the chief justice, and three lawyers appointed by lawyers' professional associations. Committee members are appointed for three-year terms, and their names and biographies are made public. The committee's mandate requires that its composition "reflect the diversity of Ontario's population, including gender, geography, racial and cultural minorities." When there are judicial vacancies, the committee advertises for qualified lawyers with at least ten years of experience to apply. The advertisements specify that "applicants must have a sound knowledge of the law, an understanding of the social issues of the day and an appreciation for the cultural diversity of Ontario ... Applications are encouraged from women, aboriginal peoples, francophones, persons with disabilities, and visible and ethnocultural minorities" (Ontario Judicial Appointments Advisory Committee 2004). After interviewing the leading applicants, the committee provides at least two names to the attorney general, who makes the final selection (although the attorney general may ask for additional names).

The qualities the committee looks for when recommending judicial appointments are daunting: professional excellence, experience in professional activities related to important legal issues and the administration of justice (including alternative dispute resolution), good writing skills, commitment to public service, awareness of social problems and values relevant to litigation, good listening skills, respect for human dignity, politeness, high ethical standards, patience, fairness, punctuality, good work habits, compassion, and humility. As will be shown in Chapter 3, the selection system implemented by Scott has gone far to make the Ontario judiciary more representative of the demographic characteristics of the province.

Three other provinces have judicial appointments committees with a recruitment as well as a screening function: Manitoba, British Columbia, and Quebec. The Manitoba Judicial Nominating Committee consists of two judges, two lawyers, and three lay persons, and it provides the attorney general with a list of three to six qualified candidates to choose from for each judicial vacancy. British Columbia has a nine-member Judicial Council of four lay persons, three judges, and two lawyers, which, among other duties, recruits and screens nominees for judicial appointments. Whenever a judicial vacancy occurs at the provincial level in Quebec, there are public advertisements for applicants, and a three-person committee composed of a judge, a lawyer, and a lay person is struck to screen the applicants. Several other provinces provide for some lay participation in the screening of nominations for judicial appointments. In Alberta, for example, the six-member Judicial Council screens nominations for judgeships; it consists of three judges, one lawyer, and two others who may be lay persons. New Brunswick has ten judicial appointment "advisors," two of whom are lay persons. These ten never meet as a group, but provide individual comments about judicial applicants, which the attorney general is given the opportunity to consider (Friedland 1995, ch. 11).

At the federal level, beginning in 1988 the government of Brian Mulroney set up judicial appointment advisory committees in each province and territory to recommend candidates for the superior courts and courts of appeal. (This replaced the judicial appointments screening system established by Pierre Trudeau, in which a committee of the Canadian Bar Association reviewed the suitability of judicial appointees being considered by the minister of justice.) In 1994, three regional committees were established in Ontario, and two in Quebec. At present, each federal judicial appointments advisory committee consists of three lay members, three lawyers, and one judge (Office of the Commissioner for Federal Judicial Affairs 2005). The Mulroney reforms were not as far-reaching as far as those in Ontario. The federal committees have a minority of lay members, and instead of serving a recruitment function, as in Ontario, the federal committees merely screen candidates presented to them by the commissioner for federal judicial affairs. As well, the names of the federal committee members are not published, which weakens the public accountability of the process.

The federal committees merely designate applicants as "highly recommended," "recommended," or "unable to recommend." Thus, there is still large scope for the minister of justice, if he or she chooses to do so, to skew appointments in the direction of supporters of the party in power. In fact, although patronage in federal judicial appointments may not be as rampant as it was prior to the 1988 reforms, lawyers who support the party in power may still have a significantly better chance of obtaining a federal judicial appointment (Russell and Ziegel 1991). It should be noted that in 2005, the Martin government was considering improvements to the federal system of judicial appointments.

As a rule of thumb, two-thirds to three-quarters of the judges sitting on the provincial and territorial courts of appeal, the Federal Court of Appeal, and the Supreme Court of Canada have been elevated from lower courts. As well, up to 5 percent of the judges on the superior trial courts have been elevated from the provincial courts. None of the judges who have been elevated have been screened by any appointments committee in relation to their elevation. Decisions about promotions are made by the minister of justice with advice from the commissioner for federal judicial affairs, and there is often consultation between the minister of justice, the chief justice of the court concerned, and the provincial attorney general. Sometimes judges hoping for a promotion make their desires known to the minister; at other times a promotion comes as a complete surprise. Very little is known about the decision-making process in the minister's office that leads to judicial promotions, and except for the fact that the minister has been elected to the House of Commons, there is no public participation in these decisions. Martin Friedland, who prepared a report on judicial independence and accountability for the Canadian Judicial Council, recommended that a committee that includes lay persons should be set up to advise regarding all elevations, including appointments to the Supreme Court of Canada (Friedland 1995, 255-60).

Devising appropriate selection procedures for the Supreme Court of Canada requires careful consideration. Pierre Trudeau, both as justice minister and then as prime minister, was determined to remove partisan political considerations altogether from the calculus for his ten appointments to the Supreme Court. He did his best to appoint top-quality judges regardless of their past political involvement, although he most certainly took into account potential candidates' reputations regarding federalism and human rights issues (McCormick 2000). Bora Laskin, for example, was surprised to be offered an appointment to the Supreme Court by Trudeau, as he did not have the kind of political connections with the party in power that Supreme Court appointees had often had. And Jean Beetz, known to be strong on provincial rights, was nevertheless appointed by Trudeau because of his excellent academic reputation. Subsequent prime ministers have tried to maintain a nonpartisan approach to Supreme Court appointments, and despite occasional complaints that partisan considerations were factors for some Mulroney and Chrétien appointees, generally Supreme Court appointments since the beginning of the Trudeau era have been widely praised for their quality.

Until recently, little was known about the process by which the prime minister, with the assistance of the minister of justice and his or her officials, decided to fill vacancies on the Supreme Court. In 2004 Justice Minister Irwin Cotler, in testimony before the House of Commons Justice Committee, outlined the nature of the process that had tended to occur (Cotler 2004a). Regional considerations come first. There are by law three judges from Quebec, and there are usually three from Ontario, two from the West, and one from the Atlantic region. When there is a vacancy on the Court, the replacement usually has to be appointed from the same region as that of the retiring judge. The justice minister said that to identify candidates, the minister would consult with, among others, the chief justice of Canada and sometimes other Supreme Court judges, the attorney general and chief justices of the courts from the relevant region, and one or more senior members of the law society and the bar association from that region. Once a list of candidates is established, the minister consults with the prime minister to consider the merit of each candidate. The three criteria identified by Cotler were professional capacity (including proficiency in the law), personal characteristics (including integrity, patience, and reliability), and diversity. Cotler also mentioned that officials in the Department of Justice prepared "jurisprudential profiles" on the candidates, which evaluated the quality of the decisions of candidates with a judicial track record.

If the system of appointments to the Supreme Court was working fairly well, why did Prime Minister Paul Martin promise to reform it as part of his attack on the "democratic deficit"? During the 2004 election campaign, Martin argued that in a democracy, MPs deserve some role in the selection of Supreme Court judges. And Justice Minister Cotler commented, "The public has the right to know what we do now about the appointment of Supreme Court judges ... Canadians ... may feel that [the appointment] process is secretive, and if it's secretive, it's partisan" (*National Post,* 31 December 2003, A15). These are persuasive arguments, but reforming the procedure for Supreme Court appointments is trickier than it might first appear, and hastily implementing an inadequate selection process might be worse than leaving the old system in place.

Shortly after winning the June 2004 election, the Martin government was faced with the necessity of replacing two retiring Supreme Court judges. The Commons Justice Committee heard about appropriate selection procedures from a number of experts, including Peter Russell, who warned of the dangers of adopting a poorly thought-out process. In the end, the government decided to adopt an interim procedure in order to ensure that the Supreme Court would be up to full strength for its fall term in 2004. An ad hoc committee was established to review the government's two nominations to the Court, Ontario Court of Appeal judges Rosalie Abella and Louise Charron. The committee included seven MPs (three Liberal, two Conservative, one Bloc Québécois, and one NDP), a representative of the Law Society of Upper Canada, and the chief justice of the Federal Court representing the Canadian Judicial Council. Justice Minister Cotler appeared before the committee to describe the consultations that had led to the two nominations, and to present biographies of the nominees. Opposition members of the ad hoc committee complained that they were given very little time to research the backgrounds of the two nominees, and that consultation with the committee was pro forma and had done nothing to make the selection process more democratic. They have a point. What kind of process would work more effectively?

Alternatives suggested by Jacob Ziegel (1999) are the creation of a nominating committee that would present short lists of candidates to the prime minister as vacancies arise, and a public confirmation procedure for nominees of the prime minister conducted jointly by the Senate and House of Commons. Ziegel argues that both innovations would be helpful, but that a public confirmation procedure would be particularly useful because it would help to educate both parliamentarians and the public about the quality of candidates before their appointment, and might occasionally prevent an unwise appointment. The confirmation procedure would give MPs a role in overseeing the selection of judges likely to have an impact on government policy through their decisions on constitutional law issues, and would help to remind parliamentarians of the importance of the separation of powers between the judiciary on the one hand, and the legislature and executive on the other. Ziegel reminds us that if candidates are to be questioned about personal issues, this could occur in camera, as is now the case in the US Senate in the wake of the unsavoury public hearings concerning Robert Bork and Clarence Thomas.

Another approach would be to strike a search committee to recommend to the prime minister one or more candidates for Supreme Court vacancies, as they arise. Such a procedure might build on the strengths of both the nominating committee proposal and the confirmation hearing proposal, and avoid some of their weaknesses. For example, the search committee might include the minister of justice (or designate), the leader of the Opposition (or designate), the chair of the Commons Justice Committee, a nominee of the premier of the relevant province, a representative of the Canadian Bar Association, a retired Supreme Court justice, and several nonlawyers chosen to represent the interests of the public. (These lay members might be selected, for example, by a Senate committee that could request nominations from the public.)

The search committee would publish a list of desirable qualities for the new Supreme Court judge, and issue a general call for nominations. The search committee would contact those who appeared to meet the qualifications, request their permission to be considered, and create a short list of no more than five candidates. The search committee would then consult referees, interview each of the candidates, and issue a confidential report recommending one or more candidates to the prime minister. The prime minister, as head of the elected government, would make the final selection, and would be free to reject the committee's recommendations and request a new search. This approach would allow for parliamentary and public input into the judicial selection process for the Supreme Court. In 2005, Justice Minister Cotler announced a new selection process to fill an impending vacancy on the Supreme Court, but this process was interrupted by the fall of the Martin government. What Cotler had in mind was similar to what was suggested above. He would have invited members of the legal community and the public to help create a short list of up to eight candidates. An ad hoc advisory committee would have been set up that included an MP from each party, a retired judge, a lawyer, a representative of the provincial attorneys general, and two lay members. This committee would have narrowed the short list to three candidates, and the prime minister would have made the final selection.

It is disappointing that public participation is currently rather limited regarding the selection of Canadian judges. (For similar reasons, there is even less public participation in the judicial disciplinary processes discussed in Chapter 4.) This lack of participation is understandable given the historical context of the authority to make judicial appointments. Another obstacle to greater lay participation in the justice system may be society's lack of respect for the good sense in legal matters of citizens who are not lawyers, and excessive deference to lawyers. It is encouraging, however, that during the last dozen years of the twentieth century, judicial selection or judicial screening committees to promote more meritorious appointments became generally institutionalized with regard to all levels of court, and lay participation in these committees in order to represent the public interest has become accepted as a given in the democratic context. Only in Ontario are lay members currently in the majority, however; in the other jurisdictions, recommendations for judicial appointments remain primarily the preserve of the legal profession. This is not to argue that the legal profession cannot represent the public interest, but merely to point out that like any association, it might be prone to put its collegial interests ahead of the public interest when there is a conflict.

Public Participation through Citizen Monitoring: The "Open Court" Concept

Court proceedings are generally open to the public so that members of the public can see for themselves whether justice is being done. The open court concept is a reaction to secret court proceedings, made infamous by the Star Chamber court of Henry VIII, where enemies of the government could be put on trial secretly so that due process would not have to be followed.

Thanks to the open court, newspapers assign court reporters to follow the trials that they think will be of greatest interest to their readers. Although dramatic or gory allegations of criminal wrongdoing usually dominate the resulting articles, any slip-ups by judges, prosecutors, or defence lawyers are also reported. No doubt, the possibility of being embarrassed in media reports helps to promote higher standards.

Canadian schoolchildren usually make at least one class visit to a court, and court visits are common assignments in law-related classes in universities and colleges. Political scientists who study the courts are grateful that the open court concept facilitates their research projects. As well, there are organized "court watcher" groups whose members monitor particular kinds of court activities such as the treatment of women as witnesses or as victims in sexual assault cases. The friends and relatives of litigants will sometimes attend hearings in order to show moral support, and some members of the general public like to attend court to watch sensational trials. But in general, most members of the public do not take advantage of the open court, and rely on the media and other groups to monitor the courts.

There are exceptions to the open court principle. The media are prohibited from publishing the names of young offenders (defendants under the age of eighteen accused of all but the most serious crimes), because there is hope that young people may more easily become rehabilitated if not branded by their peers and others as "criminals." As well, accused persons or victims may request the judge to order a closed hearing or to impose a publication ban in some trials, for example, in cases involving sexual assault, or when the publicity about the trial may negatively affect the reputation of the litigants or witnesses. Similarly, where either the Crown or the defence fears that publicity about the case may make it difficult or impossible to find or keep an impartial jury, a judge may be requested to order a publication ban on the details of the preliminary hearing or of the jury trial itself. All of these limits to the concept of an open court are violations of freedom of expression as guaranteed by the Charter of Rights, but through litigation they have all been found, within bounds, to constitute reasonable limits to freedom of expression in the context of a democratic society.

In a democratic society, where respect for individual rights is valued, it is not always easy to decide whose rights should predominate when there is a conflict. For example, 10 to 20 percent of criminal accused persons are found not guilty at trial. Is it fair that the names of adult accused persons should be published, possibly ruining their reputations even when they are found to be not guilty? Max Wyman, former president of the University of Alberta, has argued that publication bans ought to be the rule rather than the exception unless a person is found guilty, because in a democracy, the right to privacy should usually outweigh the right of the media to publicize what may amount to gossip (Gall 2004, 185). On the other hand, publication bans can also be used to suppress information of great public importance, as seems to have been the case regarding a trial that took place in secret between 2000 and 2003 in Toronto. When an application by the *Globe and Mail* and the CBC resulted in the trial becoming open, it was revealed that former prime minister Brian Mulroney had accepted $300,000 from German businessman Karlheinz Schreiber shortly after leaving office (Kaplan 2004). This is information that the Canadian public had a right to know much earlier.

Whether or not you agree with Wyman's argument, the point is that the open court concept as a tool for accountability is haphazard. Only a small fraction of cases are actually scrutinized by members of the public who are there to ensure that justice is done, or by the media. Public participation in the governance of courts is likely to be a more effective accountability mechanism.

Public Participation in the Administration of Courts

The tendency for the courts to be inward looking rather than public serving is one of their legacies as predemocratic institutions. Since Peter Russell observed in 1975 that "judging is still not regarded as the provision of a basic social service" (p. 88) by many judges and lawyers, there have been some modest moves toward recognizing the value of public input. Effective mechanisms need to be found to ensure that the concerns of the public about unnecessary delays, disrespectful treatment of witnesses and litigants, and cumbersome and unnecessary procedures are heard and addressed. Absent such public input, courts have little incentive to improve their standards.

Court administration, which includes providing courthouses, court staff, and tools for case scheduling, is the responsibility of the executive branch of government. As noted in Chapter 1, the Constitution gives the provinces the responsibility for the administration of all courts including those with federally appointed judges, except for the purely federal courts (the Supreme Court of Canada, the Federal Courts, and the Tax Court). In most provinces, the courts are administered as a branch of the provincial attorney general's department; in Quebec, the relevant ministry is the Justice Department. Those Canadians with complaints about the administration of justice, or suggestions for its improvement, can voice their demands to the provincial attorney general (or minister of justice in Quebec), or to their elected members. My impression, however, is that very few lay persons contact the appropriate minister with their views about problems in court administration, except during times of unusually lengthy backlogs of cases. This reticence of the public to complain is partly because people may not know who is responsible for court administration (many assume that the judges are), and partly because of the aura of courts as being the preserve of judges and lawyers, where public input does not seem appropriate.

Lawyers' associations, however, do tend to provide the minister with fairly regular commentaries about issues in court administration. These associations include the provincial law societies, which are the governing bodies of the law profession, the Canadian Bar Association and its provincial branches, and various advocates' societies (organizations for civil litigation lawyers) and associations of lawyers representing criminal accused persons. The recommendations of these associations tend to be given careful consideration by the minister and his or her advisors because of the influence that lawyers have in politics. To the extent that lawyers represent the views of their clients rather than just their own professional interests, lawyerly influence provides an indirect form of public input.

During the 1970s, advancing urbanization and related social changes led to increasing backlogs of cases in large population centres across Canada, and an unusually high number of complaints from the public. Many of these complaints were sent to judges because of the general assumption that judges are in charge of administering courts. Thus in the late 1970s, some Canadian judges developed a fair degree of interest in taking over responsibility for court administration. If the judges were going to get the blame for problems in court administration, they reasoned, they may as well take responsibility for fixing them. In 1979 the Canadian Judicial Council (composed of all the superior court chief justices and associate chief justices in Canada) and various provincial court judges' associations passed resolutions supporting more judicial involvement in court administration. As a result, the council requested Quebec's chief justice, Jules Deschênes, to investigate.

Deschênes's main recommendation, published in 1981 after an exhaustive tour of Canadian courts, was that the administration of all courts should be transferred to judges. He suggested a ten-year transition period when administrative systems would move from consultation with judges to decision sharing, and finally to the complete independence of the courts administratively. Most important from the perspective of democracy, he recommended that citizens' advisory committees be established in every province to ensure that the concerns of the public could be heard, and so that representatives of the public could participate in finding solutions. The Canadian Judicial Council was not enthusiastic about Deschênes's recommendations, simply concluding that the government ought to consult the judiciary about administrative matters. Some judges felt that increased involvement in administration would compromise their independence. As well, a number of judges were skeptical that lay persons could offer useful input into resolving administrative issues.

In 1987, in the course of making sweeping recommendations regarding the reorganization of Ontario courts into administrative regions, Mr. Justice Thomas Zuber recommended the establishment of courts management advisory committees including judges, administrators, members of the bar, other stakeholders in the justice system, and lay persons representing the general public. These committees would exist at the provincial level and also in each of seven regions of the province. The committees were established by law, but their effectiveness has been mixed. In some of Ontario's regions, they are regarded as indispensable mechanisms for identifying issues, especially from the public's perspective, and for finding solutions that work. In other regions, the committees are regarded as a waste of time. Three problems have tended to undermine the unsuccessful committees. Some committees have been unable to overcome the natural friction among the various stakeholder groups in the courts, some have members whose personalities interfere with collegial processes, and those chairing meetings have not always possessed the skills required to conduct an effective meeting. As well, the effectiveness of the lay representation on the committees depends on the personal qualities of the lay members, and it appears that some attorneys general may not have given serious enough consideration to the appointment of the lay members.

Peter Russell's observation that the courts tend to be regarded by judges and lawyers as the place where they practise their "private professional craft" is still largely accurate (1975, 88). A few very modest advances have been made, however, in providing for more effective public input into the administration of justice, at least in Ontario. Clearly, the "democratization" of court administration through allowing greater public input remains a challenge as well as an important goal in the twenty-first century.

Participation in Court Proceedings

Members of the public participate in court proceedings primarily as litigants: by invoking the courts to settle a dispute, or by being forced to defend themselves when taken to court by someone else. They also participate as witnesses, jurors, intervenors, and expert witnesses. From the perspective of this democratic audit, the key questions concern the nature of this participation. Is participation meaningful, and are participants treated with respect?

Participation as Litigants and Witnesses

According to a fax from Statistics Canada, nearly half a million criminal code cases were heard in Canadian courts during 2001-2. There were probably an equal number of non-criminal code, provincial offence cases. On the civil side, Statistics Canada does not yet have accurate data on the number of civil cases that go to court. The Ministry of the Attorney General for Ontario publishes an annual report of its court statistics, the *Court Statistics Annual Report*. If these data are indicative of the Canadian situation it appears that more than 500,000 cases are filed annually across Canada and nearly half are small claims cases (Ontario 1999-2000, no. A-26). Nonetheless, only about a tenth of the civil cases filed, not including the small claims cases, ever get on the trial list, and only a quarter of those that get on the trial list get to trial. The great majority of civil cases are settled out of court or never pursued by the initiating party. But the rate of appeal for civil cases – 3 percent – is far higher than the 0.4 percent for criminal cases, perhaps because the lower standard of proof in civil cases makes a successful appeal seem more likely, and because of the potential financial consequences of not appealing (Greene et al. 1998).

In a democracy, all who come into contact with the justice system deserve to be treated with respect, including those accused of breaking the law. Thus, accused persons are to be presumed innocent until proven guilty before an independent and impartial tribunal, and according to a process in which accused persons can fully and fairly present evidence in their defence. Sections 7 to 14 of the Charter of Rights and Freedoms, the "legal rights" sections, represent a kind of code of conduct for the fair treatment of accused persons in criminal proceedings.

The legal rights sections of the Charter of Rights constitute one of the most extensive sets of guidelines for ensuring the fair treatment of criminal accused persons in the world. The drafters of the Charter were able to take advantage of the historical development of protections for accused persons in the Anglo-Canadian common law system, which had been included in the 1960 Canadian Bill of Rights. As well, several "new" legal rights were added to the Charter that developed out of Justice Minister Trudeau's amendments to the Criminal Code in the mid-1960s. These additions include the right to a trial within a reasonable time, the right not to be subjected to unreasonable search and seizure, the prohibition of retroactive criminalization of actions (other than war crimes), the right not to be tried and punished more than once for the same offence, the right to the lesser punishment if the punishment for an offence changes after a person committed the offence in question, the right to be informed of the right to counsel, and the right to a jury trial for offences carrying a potential sentence of five years or more. The absence of public pressure to add new legal rights to the Charter since 1982 is an indication that, for the moment, the legal rights protections in the Charter are probably adequate. Some have expressed concerns, however, that some parts of the federal government's antiterrorism legislation, Bill C-36, do not protect adequately the rights of those suspected of terrorist activities who are, in fact, innocent, and that the protections of the Charter may not resolve this potential issue (Roach 2003; Daniels, Macklem, and Roach 2001).

How effective are the legal rights sections of the Charter in promoting respect for the rights of criminal accused persons? There is evidence that in the courtroom itself, the majority of criminal accused persons believe that their lawyers acted appropriately to defend their rights, and that the judges did their best to make fair decisions, even when these decisions went against the accused. Most complaints that criminal accused persons have about the justice system concern the often excruciating length of time between arrest and either conviction or acquittal (Tufts 2002; Peter McCormick and I also found this in our Alberta interviews in the 1980s).

Unfortunately, very little research has been conducted with regard to the attitudes of litigants in civil cases. At the beginning of the twenty-first century, the Canadian Forum on Civil Justice, located at the University of Alberta Faculty of Law, began to study the Canadian civil justice system in a systematic way. Preliminary results indicate that litigants frequently encounter difficulties in communicating effectively with the civil justice system (Lowe, Stratton, and Tsui, 2004).

Those called as witnesses in both civil and criminal cases are usually quite willing to contribute to the justice system by giving evidence. When they get to court, witnesses I have interviewed most often considered that the judge listened to what they had to say and treated them with respect. But witnesses in both civil and criminal cases have two common complaints about their participation in the trial process: lengthy and unnecessary delays, and unpleasant cross-examinations.

Trials are never scheduled for the convenience of witnesses, and most have to take time off work or other daily commitments in order to comply with a summons to appear in court to give evidence. A witness may wait most of the day in order to present evidence, often for five minutes or less. Moreover, cases are commonly adjourned once or twice, and occasionally more often, either because some of the other witnesses are not present, or because one of the parties is not prepared to go ahead. There is rarely an apology to the witnesses for long waits, or for having to return to court a second or third or fourth time.

Many delays of this nature, which add to the suffering of litigants and sour the experience of witnesses who are usually otherwise quite willing to do their public duty and appear in court, could probably be avoided (Millar and Baar 1982; Solomon and Somerlot 2000). Delays occur for a number of reasons. The most common reason, according to my interviews, relates to the bad habits of some trial lawyers, and the unwillingness or inability of judges to curb these tendencies. Some lawyers are willing to delay a criminal case in the interests of their clients for as long as possible, with the hope that witnesses for the prosecution will eventually get discouraged and fail to appear, or that they'll move and then can't be issued a summons. If witnesses do appear in spite of a long delay, they will be easier to trip up in cross-examination because of the impact of elapsed time on memory. Other trial lawyers take on too many cases, and therefore have to request adjournments in some cases in order to attend other hearings. Yet other trial lawyers, according to some judges, are not prepared to proceed with a case because of their work habits: they've left the preparation too late.

Cross-examinations are often another source of annoyance for witnesses. A time-honoured strategy of lawyers is to cast doubt on the arguments presented by the other side by trying to destroy the credibility of its witnesses. This sometimes means sharp questions intended to rattle the equanimity of a witness so that he or she will say something that casts doubt on the testimony. This kind of treatment sometimes seems insulting, and can leave a bad impression of the court experience. As well, witnesses sometimes do not feel they are allowed to tell the whole of their story that is relevant to the case. For example, witnesses are sometimes told that they must answer "yes" or "no" to a question when they think that the answer is a bit of both.

In our court system, litigants have a right to be heard, and parties to a dispute have the right at trial to present evidence without arbitrary time limits. From that perspective, the Canadian court system clearly respects the right of litigants and witnesses to participate in litigation. Nevertheless, procedures for getting at the truth that rely unnecessarily on attempts to discredit the other side mean that litigants and witnesses may come away from court feeling angry and disrespected. Perhaps this explains why those who have come into contact with the justice system tend to have a less positive view of the courts than those who have not (Statistics Canada 1999). Finally, unnecessary delays, as well as the cost of litigation, interfere with the ability to participate effectively.

Public Input into Verdicts: The Jury System

The jury system is often referred to as a great democratizing mechanism for the court because it allows for public input into decisions about guilt and innocence: "jury service provides one of the few opportunities for the citizen in a representative democracy to participate directly in government decision-making" (Russell 1987, 274). The principle behind jury trials is that in serious criminal cases and in liability cases where large sums of money are involved, citizens have the right to have their guilt or liability determined by their equals. As well, citizen participation is considered to help promote fairness and accountability. All Canadians over eighteen are eligible to be called for jury duty unless they are members of exempted groups, such as the police and medical doctors (Granger 1996). Jury trials occur only in the provincial superior trial courts. About 2 percent of all criminal cases across all courts are determined through a jury trial (Russell 1987, 274, 275), although about 40 percent of the trials for serious indictable offences in superior courts are jury trials (Vidmar 1999). The rate of use of jury trials in civil cases varies widely among provinces from 3 to 10 percent except in Ontario, where about 20 percent of civil cases involve jury trials – mostly suits resulting from motor vehicle accidents (Bogart 1999).

Jury selection is an arduous process. In Toronto, for example, about 30,000 persons, or 1.5 percent of adult citizens, are sent jury duty notices each year. From this initial list, a cohort of 500 people is required to report to the courthouse every second week (except in summer) in case they're needed (and many are not). Potential jurors are questioned by the lawyers for both sides under a judge's supervision. Lawyers for either side may object to and exclude particular jurors because they speculate that their background might cause them to be biased with regard to the case at hand. As well, the Crown can object to up to four jurors for no reason at all, and the accused's lawyer has the right to between four and twenty such challenges, depending on the seriousness of the charge (Hogg 2004, 7.1(h)). During the jury selection process, some counsel clearly have no desire to select a truly impartial jury, but rather one that is likely to be partial to their side.

Since colonial times, the incidence of jury trials has been steadily declining. This is partly because judges are now much more highly qualified than before, partly because of the expense of jury trials, and partly because there are often more opportunities to appeal the decisions of judges than those of juries. (No written decisions from jury trials can be challenged on appeal.) Although the Charter of Rights guarantees that anyone charged with an offence that carries at least a five-year prison term has a right to a trial by jury, many accused persons opt for a trial by a judge alone. A trial by judge alone can often be scheduled sooner than a jury trial, and some accused persons fear that a jury is less likely to be impartial than a judge.

An accused person who wants to delay the time to trial may opt for a trial by jury, thus getting a trial date further in the future, and then change his or her mind and opt for either a trial or a guilty plea in front of a judge alone, thus delaying the process even further (Russell 1987, 275). The inconvenience caused to potential jurors who must wait at the courthouse in case they are selected for jury duty, and the misuse of the jury system by lawyers who try to construct a biased jury or hope to delay proceedings, seem to indicate that the democratizing impact of the jury system is sometimes counterbalanced by abusive tactics.

The jury system may be at a crossroads. It should either be reformed to ensure that juries are truly representative of the community and as impartial as possible, and to ensure that abuses of the system are eliminated, or it should be abolished. Abolition of jury trials in criminal cases would require an amendment to the Charter of Rights with the support of seven provinces (including either Ontario or Quebec) and Parliament, and so reform is the preferred option. However, "Law Reform Commission reports and scholarly publications contain a plethora of recommendations, few of which have been acted upon" (Russell 1987, 278). What is required is the political will to save the jury system and ensure that its democratic potential is realized.

Public Input into Adjudication

Three fairly recent developments have opened new avenues for public input into adjudicative decisions that affect government policies. First, during the 1970s and 1980s the Supreme Court broadened the rules of standing, making it easier for those wishing to challenge a government policy to do so before a judge (Russell 1987, 356). A person with legal standing in a case has a close enough connection with a legally contestable matter to bring a suit in his or her own name.

Second, the Supreme Court opened the door more widely for intervenors to present arguments in policy-related cases. Intervenors are parties not directly involved in a dispute who wish to present arguments to the court because they have an interest in the policy implications of the litigation. The most frequent intervenors are the provincial and federal governments, because they have a right to intervene in constitutional cases and an interest in their outcome. In addition, a number of public interest groups were formed during the last few decades of the twentieth century to attempt to impact public policy through litigation. The best-known of these groups are the Canadian Civil Liberties Association (CCLA), the Women's Legal Education and Action Fund (LEAF), the National Citizens Coalition (NCC), and various Aboriginal groups (Young and Everitt 2004).

Third, the Supreme Court's Anti-Inflation Act reference decision of 1976 signalled a new willingness of Canadian judges to consider social science and historical evidence. Before this time, although the so-called Brandeis brief had been commonplace in the United States since 1908, evidence from social scientists and historians had been viewed with suspicion by Canadian judges. This was because such evidence was often based on interviews, which according to a conservative interpretation of the rules of evidence were "hearsay." (Lawyer Louis Brandeis defended the constitutionality of an Oregon law that limited the hours of work for female laundry workers by including in his brief, reference to data from medical and sociological journals. This was probably the first time that social science evidence had been admitted in a common law country. Brandeis won his case before the US Supreme Court in 1908.)

PUBLIC INTEREST LITIGATION

It is sometimes argued that one way in which the courts can be more responsive to input from the general public regarding constitutional issues, and thereby overcome the tendency to be too inward focused on the views of legal professionals, is to welcome the applications of intervenors in cases that might have a significant impact on public policy. In fact, the number of intervenors accepted by the Supreme Court increased steadily until 2001, and then levelled off (Monahan 2002).

One of the weaknesses of the argument that intervenors help democratize the litigation process is that significant obstacles must be surmounted to obtain intervenor status. They obviously exceed those in the way of lobbying an elected legislator or a bureaucrat. The requirements for knowledge of cases being litigated that are relevant to the average citizen, money, and organizational prerequisites all help to account for the relatively small number of intervenors. As well, as Morton and Knopff (2000) show, intervenors tend to represent a relatively narrow area of specialized interests. The large number of "one shot" intervenors suggests that their lack of experience might jeopardize their effectiveness (McCormick 1995).

A study conducted by Gregory Hein (2000) of the activity of public interest groups in the Supreme Court of Canada and the Federal Court between 1988 and 1998 shows that there were 819 instances where advocacy groups either constituted a party to a dispute or intervened. The majority of these involvements were by corporate interests (468), and the remainder were noncorporate interest groups such as Aboriginal peoples (77) and "Charter Canadians" (80) – such as advocates for the mentally handicapped, the elderly, or gays and lesbians, whose members often felt marginalized by the political process prior to the Charter of Rights. Hein concludes that interest group involvement has been generally positive for Canadian democracy by allowing input into the policy process by previously marginalized groups. As well, businesses are "pushed into court by the changing circumstances that make litigation a compelling strategic manoeuvre" (1). Although there are clearly disadvantages to interest group litigation, Hein concludes that because the judicial system "responds to a diverse range of interests," interest group activity in the courts "should be celebrated" (2).

In the mid-1990s, my colleagues and I asked Canadian appellate court judges whether it was appropriate for social and public interest groups to use the courts to achieve social change. The appellate court judges were about evenly divided on this issue. Some saw the activity of interest groups as enhancing democracy in an age when the pursuit of change through elected representatives seems increasingly difficult, and others saw this activity as a threat to judicial independence because it took the courts outside of their proper sphere. Supreme Court of Canada judges were, on the whole, somewhat more open to the activity of public interest groups, one specifically mentioning benefits to democracy (Greene et al. 1998).

Expert Witnesses

When social scientists or historians present expert evidence in court that is either representative of a more general set of public attitudes, or that helps to further the public interest as part of the litigation process, then the expert witness can, in a sense, become a proxy for the public interest. The cases in which expert witnesses actually serve to represent the public interest are likely few and far between, as most experts are "hired guns" carefully chosen to represent the interests of a litigant, which may be contrary to the public interest. Nevertheless, in some situations the views of a broader public can be represented through an expert's evidence.

Three cases help to illustrate the strengths and weakness of expert witnesses acting as proxies for the public interest in litigation. These are the *Ford* case on the language of outdoor signs in Quebec, the *Askov* case on unreasonable delay in litigation, and the *Marshall* case on Native fishing rights in the Maritimes.

Ford v. Quebec (A.G.) (1988)

In 1977 the National Assembly in Quebec, controlled by a Parti Québécois government, enacted Bill 101, the Charter of the French Language. This legislation, among other things, outlawed the use of English and other languages on most outdoor commercial signs in Quebec. Many francophones were worried about the possibility of assimilation into the English-speaking world, given the low birth rate of native Québécois and high immigration levels. The thinking was that in order to encourage new immigrants to assimilate with the francophone community, all of Quebec, especially Montreal, needed a "French look." Bill 101 was intended to accomplish this goal by ensuring that signs on businesses would be in French only. But in 1984 several merchants opposed to the signs policy, including Valerie Ford, requested a declaration from the Quebec Superior Court that parts of Bill 101 contravened the Quebec Charter of Rights and the Canadian Charter of Rights.

The issue for which expert evidence was key was the question of whether the violation of freedom of expression contained in Bill 101 could be justified as a "reasonable limit" to rights. The attorney general of Quebec referred to several sociological and linguistic studies that he claimed supported the government's position. When the case ended up in the Supreme Court, the Court's reading of the evidence led it to a different conclusion:

> The material deals with ... the vulnerable position of the French language in Quebec and Canada ... The material amply establishes the importance of the legislative purpose reflected in the Charter of the French Language and that it is a response to a substantial and pressing need ... The threat to the French language demonstrated to the government that it should, in particular, take steps to assure that the "visage linguistique" of Quebec would reflect the predominance of the French language. The ... materials do not, however, demonstrate that the requirement of the use of French only is either necessary for the achievement of the legislative objective or proportionate to it (777-9).

The court concluded that although the Quebec legislature was justified in taking action to ensure that the "visage linguistique" in Quebec would be primarily francophone, the social science evidence did not support the necessity of banning other languages on outdoor signs. The sociolinguistic studies supported only ensuring that French was predominant.

As a proxy for the public interest, the social science evidence effectively represented the legitimate fears of francophones about the erosion of their language through demographic changes. But while the desire of most francophones, as expressed through their elected representatives, was to allow only French on outdoor signs, the social science evidence showed that such a far-reaching ban was not necessary to achieve the objective of maintaining the predominance of the French language in Quebec. If democracy is thought of as including both effective participation and respect for minority rights, the proxy representation of both majority and minority interests through social science evidence appears to have succeeded.

R. v. Askov (1990)

The Charter of Rights states, "Any person charged with an offence has the right to be tried within a reasonable time" (s. 11(b)). The first major decision about the meaning of this section was the *Askov* decision of 1990. In November 1983 in the Peel region east of Toronto, Elijah Askov and several others were charged with conspiracy to commit extortion and weapons offences. Their trial did not begin until September 1986, nearly three years after the original charges were laid. Counsel for the accused persons requested and received a stay of proceedings on the grounds that the right to trial within a reasonable time had been violated. That decision was appealed to the Supreme Court, which released its decision in 1990.

Counsel for Askov had submitted social science evidence compiled by Carl Baar, then head of Canada's only graduate program in judicial administration. Baar's data showed that delays in Peel County were among the lengthiest in North America, and that courts elsewhere in Canada and the United States were capable of bringing cases of the same degree of complexity as Askov's to trial in a much shorter time. Mr. Justice Peter Cory, writing for the Court, noted Baar's observation that "if Canadian courts were required to set cases for trial within six months, they could almost universally do so." Cory noted the harm caused by unnecessarily long delays: witnesses tend to forget what they witnessed or to disappear, victims suffer because of lack of closure, and the public becomes disillusioned with the justice system. Baar's evidence confirmed the suspicions of nearly all victims of lengthy delays in the court system: cases can be brought to trial much more quickly if those responsible for court administration have the will and the resources to do so. Cory declared that henceforth, unless cases reached trial within six to eight months, there was a good possibility that the judges would find that Charter right to a trial within a reasonable time had been violated (so long as the delays had been caused by the justice system and not by the accused), and would stay proceedings.

The *Askov* decision had a major impact on prosecutions in Canadian courts where there had been long delays. Within three months, more than 12,000 cases in Ontario alone had been stayed by judges, or charges had been withdrawn by the Crown because of anticipation that the *Askov* test could not be met. New resources were put into backlogged courts to ensure that cases could come to trial within six to eight months. At first blush, it appears that social science evidence, as a proxy for accused persons suffering from unreasonable delays, was extremely successful.

The story does not end here. Although the Court's understanding of Baar's data was generally correct, and the six-to-eight-month guideline was reasonable, in some minor respects the Court misrepresented the data. As well, the Court referred to data from Montreal courts that were not in Baar's evidence, and compared these data to data from outside Quebec in inappropriate ways. These errors amounted to an invitation to Crown counsel to request a reinterpretation of *Askov*, and this occurred in the *Morin* case decided in 1992. In *Morin*, Mr. Justice John Sopinka, writing for the Court, stated that "in *Askov* we were given statistics with respect to Montreal in an affidavit by Professor Baar. Subsequently, it was brought to our attention that this was a misleading comparison" (*R. v. Morin* 1992, 797). Note, however, that Baar had not introduced the Montreal data: it is not clear where the Supreme Court got the misleading data about the Montreal delays (Baar 1993). Nevertheless, in the *Morin* decision Sopinka revised the *Askov* guideline, and announced that an eight-to-ten-month delay between the laying of charges and a trial in a provincial court would be acceptable. He then qualified this guideline with a number of considerations that would make it easier for the Crown to justify lengthier delays between arrest and trial.

Therefore, while Baar's evidence did successfully serve as a proxy for the views and interests of those suffering from unnecessary delays in the courts, the fact that judges and lawyers may lack the skills necessary to utilize social science evidence effectively may erode the value of this kind of public participation in the adjudicative process.

R. v. Marshall (1999a, b)

In the early 1990s, there were indications in the case law that the Supreme Court might be open to recognizing Aboriginal treaty rights that governments had refused to recognize (*R. v. Sparrow* 1990; *R. v. Sioui*

1990). As a result, some members of the Mi'kmaq nation in Nova Scotia decided to set up a court challenge to federal restrictions on their fishing. Donald Marshall, Jr. volunteered to get arrested for breaking the fishing regulations, because he had already been through the judicial process and was used to its trauma. (Marshall was wrongfully convicted of murder in 1971, and had spent eleven years in jail.) Marshall fished for eels without a licence during the closed season with illegal nets, and was duly arrested for violating federal fishing regulations. He admitted that he had caught and sold 463 pounds of eels without a licence, off season, and with a prohibited net. He claimed, however, that he was exempt from the fishing regulations according to treaties that the Mi'kmaq had signed with the British in 1760-1.

At the forty-day trial, the judge was presented with expert testimony from three historians: Dr. John Reid and Dr. William Wicken for Marshall, and Dr. Stephen Patterson for the Crown. The major issue in this case was whether the Crown's strict interpretation of the 1760-1 treaties should prevail, or whether the interpretation advanced by Marshall and other Mi'kmaq was more convincing. The Crown's position was that the special rights to trade mentioned in the treaties had become obsolete, and therefore the Mi'kmaq had no special trading privileges. Marshall's argument was that the Mi'kmaq understood that the treaties guaranteed their continued right to trade, and that this right to trade implied a right to trap, hunt, and fish for subsistence. Changes in trade since 1761 did not affect that right, and federal regulations would have to take these Native rights into account.

At the Supreme Court, the majority concluded that, according to the historical evidence presented in trial, in 1760 the Natives had negotiated a continuing right to earn a living through trading furs and fish for European goods, and this right is now protected by the Constitution. The Mi'kmaq are therefore entitled to earn a moderate livelihood from their fishing, hunting, and trapping. The government can regulate fishing in order to protect resources, as long as this regulation does not violate Mi'kmaq treaty rights.

In the aftermath of the *Marshall* decision, there were a number of confrontations between Native and non-Native fishers, and between

Native fishers and the federal Department of Fisheries and Oceans. A fishermen's association applied to the Supreme Court for a rehearing of the case. In dismissing the application, the Supreme Court in essence issued a clarification of its earlier decision (*R. v. Marshall* 1999b) that did little to settle the tensions. The key point is that the federal government is now required by law to take into account the perspective of Native Canadians about the treaties signed in the mid-eighteenth century. In this sense, Aboriginal peoples of the Atlantic region have not only participated in litigation through expert witness testimony, but their voices have been heard in a way that they had never been heard by government officials (Wicken 2002).

EXPERT EVIDENCE AND CONSIDERATION OF PUBLIC CONCERNS

The three cases outlined above show how evidence submitted by expert witnesses can enable the interests of a broader public to be considered in cases that are likely to have an impact on a group of people much larger than the number of individual litigants. In all three cases, social scientists or historians served, in a sense, as representatives of a larger public interest. There are, of course, both advantages and disadvantages from the perspective of democracy when academic evidence becomes part of the litigation process.

Social science and historical evidence that represents the concerns and aspirations of various groups in society sometimes serves as a valuable tool for members of the legislative and executive branches of government in the policy process (Docherty 2005). Surprisingly, however, this academic evidence may be likely to be most effectively used in the courts. Academic research is sometimes referred to by policy makers in the policy branches of government departments, by cabinet ministers and their assistants, or by legislative or parliamentary committees. Professor Baar, for example, has been consulted by the attorney general's departments in several provinces with regard to issues of case-flow management in the courts. But the way in which expert evidence is considered and weighted in the executive and legislative branches is quite different. In the political branches, expert advice is considered only if it dovetails with the agendas of elected officials or the preferences of policy makers in the public service. It is hard to imagine that historical evidence about the implications of the treaties of 1760 would have received serious consideration from personnel in the Department of Fisheries and Oceans prior to the *Marshall* decision of 1999, given the department's rigid opposition to Native rights even after the *Marshall* decision. Similarly, the academic research related to reduction of backlogs of cases in courts tended to fall on deaf ears prior to the *Askov* decision. And neither PQ nor Liberal governments in Quebec were receptive to evidence from linguists that a near-complete ban of languages other than French on outdoor signs was not necessary for the protection of the French language in Quebec, until forced to by the debate generated by the *Ford* decision.

Conversely, the courts have been severely criticized for misusing social science and historical evidence: "The courts have attracted a certain amount of criticism from professional historians for what these historians see as an occasional tendency on the part of judges to assemble a 'cut and paste' version of history" (*R. v. Marshall* 1999a, para. 37-8). And the *Askov* and *Morin* cases illustrate how judges and lawyers can stumble when confronted with complex social science data. It is not surprising that the use of social science and historical evidence in court is not always up to standard, since few judges and lawyers have training as professional historians or social scientists. Another concern is that lawyers currently have no systematic way to find and retain appropriate experts; locating experts depends very much on whom the lawyers happen to know in the academic world. And what if the evidence of the expert turns out not to be entirely favourable to a counsel's client? Academics with integrity will insist that in order to preserve their academic freedom and reputation, they must be able to describe the entire situation as they see it, and cannot submit to censorship by counsel. In the end, the value of the evidence presented by social scientists and historians as a proxy for the public interest depends on the nature of the case, the goals of the litigants, and the ethical standards and intelligence of the experts themselves, the lawyers who handle the evidence, and the judges who interpret it.

Toward More Effective Participation

Public participation in the court system can take a number of forms: involvement in judicial selection, input into court administration, and participation as litigants or witnesses, as members of juries, through public interest group litigation, or through expert witness testimony. Public input into policy regarding judicial selection and court administration is currently very limited, although some inroads were made during the last two decades of the twentieth century through lay participation on judicial selection committees and courts management committees. But this lay participation is in its infancy, and needs careful nurturing to bring it to maturity. Generally speaking, litigants and witnesses are treated respectfully by judges, and have ample opportunity to present their cases fully. Much needs to be done, however, to ensure that unnecessary delays in proceeding to trial are eliminated, and that cross-examinations are conducted with respect. And although juries remain an important avenue for public participation in the courts, steps need to be taken to ensure that the jury system is not used by some litigants as an excuse for delay, that jury selection results in panels that are as impartial as possible, and that jurors are always treated with respect and not simply as cogs in the wheels of the cumbersome machinery of justice.

Opportunities for public participation in litigation directed toward changing public policy, as opposed to the settlement of disputes regulated by civil or criminal law, are limited by the nature of the adjudicative process. Nevertheless, public interest groups have used the courts extensively in the Charter of Rights era to try to effect social change. There is extensive academic debate over whether public interest group litigation helps to enhance democracy by giving voice to previously marginalized groups, or whether it diminishes democracy by privileging narrow special interests and usurping the policy-making responsibilities of elected legislatures (Morton and Knopff 2000; Mandel 1994). These are complex questions that readers must answer for themselves. My own view is that the more possibilities there are for public participation in any of our institutions, the better. As well, the desire of some groups in society to change public policies through litigation is a reaction to the perception that participation through the legislative and executive branches of government is either unwelcome or ineffective, and that a little competition from the courts might put pressure on the other two branches of government to clean up their acts.

We have seen how the public can participate in the litigation process, when there are important issues of public policy, through the testimony of expert witnesses. These experts, through their research, can tap the opinions and concerns of particular populations. Because of the nature of the adjudicative process, evidence about policy issues submitted by expert witnesses could well have a greater impact on policy than would similar evidence submitted to a cabinet minister, a legislative committee, or the policy branch of a government department. If the expert witness has integrity and does thorough research, then he or she might act as an effective proxy for the participation of particular groups in litigation.

Clearly, there is plenty of room for improvement regarding appropriate avenues for the participation of the public in Canada's court system. The major obstacle is likely to be the inertia created by some elected politicians, some lawyers, and some judges, who think that new avenues for public participation in the courts are either not required, or contrary to their view of the democratic tradition.

CHAPTER 2

Strengths

- There is now some public participation in the selection of both federally appointed and provincially appointed judges.

- There are opportunities for public participation in the courts through the right to observe most court proceedings, and through the jury system.

- Public interest groups, some of which skilfully use expert witnesses, have provided new avenues for public input into the litigation process.

- Most Canadians are satisfied with the fairness of our justice system.

- Social science evidence can sometimes be considered more carefully and dispassionately in the judicial forum, as compared with the legislative forum.

Weaknesses

- Judicial appointment is still considered to be primarily the preserve of legal professionals, who tend to be suspicious of public input.

- The public has very little input into identifying problems or finding solutions to the day-to-day running of the courts.

- The time that litigants, witnesses, and actual or potential jurors waste because of delays or adjournments does not seem to get the same attention as considerations for the efficient use of time by lawyers and judges.

- Many Canadians who have become involved in court proceedings have some complaints about how they have been treated.

INCLUSIVENESS

3

During most of the last two millennia, those who acted as judges often held other leadership roles in government. For example, in predemocratic colonial Canada, superior judges often sat on the executive council. It is important to understand that courts – the institutions in which judges practise their trade – have a history rooted in predemocratic traditions, but it is just as crucial to appreciate how the advent of democracy has changed the nature of, and public expectations for, courts.

In predemocratic times, judges were drawn from the ruling class or the priesthood. Court support staff were often appointed from among the favourites of the judges. There was no expectation that a judgeship or a job in the courts would be potentially available to everyone born in the realm. In contrast, modern concepts of democracy prescribe that the judiciary will be selected according to merit, and that the selection process will result in a judiciary that is appropriately representative of the population as a whole. As well, it is expected that lawyers, prosecutors, and court support staff will gain their positions through merit, and that the legal profession and positions in the courts will be available to all with the appropriate credentials, regardless of their gender, ethnicity, or social background.

To expect that the judiciary will be representative of every aspect of Canadian society is not realistic. Judges are selected from the ranks of experienced lawyers, and therefore they will always be older than the average adult. As well, lawyers have one of the highest-income occupations in our society. So as long as judges are selected from among experienced lawyers, they cannot be representative of average income earners. Given these limitations, however, a democratic audit of the courts ought to indicate whether the judiciary and other personnel in the court system are as inclusive of Canadian society as practically possible. For example, the judges in a truly representative judiciary would come from families that are representative of the distribution of family incomes of the entire population. As well, a judiciary ought to be representative from the perspective of factors such as gender, race, and ethnicity.

This chapter reviews the backgrounds of lawyers and other legal professionals, judges, court support staff, and litigants to evaluate to what extent they reflect major demographic groups in Canadian society. Whenever the key groups that work in the courts, or the litigants in the courts, are not representative of the larger population, it is important to inquire further. The point is that no group ought to face systemic barriers to inclusion in any of the legal professions.

Lawyers and Other Legal Professionals

There are at least three reasons why lawyers and other legal professionals should be as representative as possible of the Canadian population. First, any child growing up in a democracy ought to be able to aspire to enter any occupation suited to his or her abilities, interests, and work habits. Second, some members of particular demographic or ethnic groups may prefer, for various reasons, to obtain legal advice from other members of the same group. Third, a judiciary composed of mature lawyers is unlikely to be representative of society if the legal profession itself is not.

Until forced to change by the human rights revolution of the 1960s and subsequent decades, the legal profession was clearly not open to all demographic and ethnic groups. Up to nearly the middle of the twentieth century, some provincial law societies prohibited certain ethnic groups from becoming members. Blacks in Ontario and Nova Scotia, and Asians in British Columbia, for example, had to fight discriminatory laws to be admitted to the bar. Even when these formal restrictions were lifted, discrimination against those not of British or French origin made it more difficult for members of other groups to become lawyers. Bora Laskin, one of Canada's finest chief justices, had difficulty finding an articling position in Toronto after he graduated from law school in the late 1930s because of his Jewish ancestry (McCormick and Greene 1990, 62). And as recently as 1990, former students of mine of Asian origin perceived that they had much greater difficulty finding articling positions than their Caucasian friends. Most law schools in Canada did not admit women until the mid-twentieth century, and even after that law school was not very hospitable to them. Madam Justice Bertha Wilson, who became the first woman to sit on the Supreme Court of Canada in 1982, related to her biographer how she came within a few seconds of deciding to withdraw from law school in her first class at Dalhousie University in 1954 because she felt out of place as the only woman in her class. Fortunately for Canada, another woman entered the class and persuaded Wilson to stay so that they could provide each other with mutual support (Anderson 2001).

Since the 1960s, recruitment policies and patterns have steadily changed not only to accommodate the applications of women and minority ethnic groups, but to encourage them. As a result, in some Canadian law schools, women now constitute more than half of the students, and the student population at these schools is more or less representative of the ethnic diversity of their regions. Canada's largest law school, Osgoode Hall at York University, has a wide-ranging affirmative action program that allows Aboriginal Canadians, members of other visible minority groups, and physically handicapped persons to choose to compete for entry into law school in a different category, where ability to succeed receives greater emphasis than past grades – which are sometimes an indication more of the limited opportunities of particular social groups than of real ability.

The current desire of most law schools in Canada to recruit a representative student body may well result in a more or less representative legal profession by 2025. At present, however, representativeness remains a challenge. Let's take a brief look at the backgrounds of Canada's lawyers, according to the most recent Statistics Canada data. For analytic purposes, Statistics Canada has grouped lawyers (members of a provincial bar association and articling law students) and Quebec notaries together. Although there are notaries public in every province, in most, notaries may perform only minor legal functions such as certifying signatures on documents. In Quebec, notaries perform many of the same functions in private law that are carried out by lawyers, except representing clients in court. (In British Columbia, notaries also have greater responsibilities than in the other common law provinces, but not the extensive responsibilities of Quebec notaries.) Hence, in the following paragraphs, the term "lawyers" refers to both lawyers and Quebec notaries.

Statistics Canada also provides data that allow us to compare the backgrounds of lawyers with those of other legal professionals – paralegals and legal secretaries. Paralegals assist lawyers with the preparation of documents or research, and represent litigants in minor cases as allowed by legislation. Legal secretaries perform clerical functions in law offices, government, or corporations. (Notaries in the common law provinces may be in either category, depending on their duties.) Paralegals and legal secretaries may or may not have a college diploma in their specialty. In 1996 Statistics Canada reported 115,420 legal professionals in Canada: 58,820 lawyers, 20,080 paralegals, and 36,520 legal secretaries (Goudreau 2002, 8, 9).

The average age of these legal professionals was forty, two years older than the average Canadian in the labour force. (The labour force used as a comparator is the "experienced" labour force, which refers to all persons who were employed or looking for work at the time of the census, but not including people who had not worked at all during the year of the census and the previous year.) Practically all the lawyers had undertaken or completed postsecondary studies, compared with 82 percent of the paralegals, 72 percent of the legal secretaries, and 58 percent of the labour force in Canada. In 1996 lawyers earned an average of $81,682, which was a 7 percent decrease from 1991, reflecting the general economic downturn of the early 1990s. Paralegals earned an average of only about $36,000 in 1996, while legal secretaries earned just over $29,000. The incomes of both of these groups had remained about the same since 1991, indicating that the incomes of the legal professionals of lower status are not as vulnerable to changing economic conditions as the incomes of lawyers.

WOMEN IN THE LEGAL PROFESSIONS

In spite of advances in recruiting women to law school during the latter part of the twentieth century, in 1996 only 31 percent of lawyers were women, compared with 46 percent of the labour force and 51 percent of the Canadian population fifteen and over. But 79 percent of the paralegals and 99 percent of the legal secretaries were women, resulting in an overall proportion of women in the legal professions of 61 percent. Thus, although the legal profession is populated predominantly by women, men tend to have the more prestigious, highest-earning positions.

On average, women in the legal sector were six years younger than their male counterparts, an indication of two trends. First, women are more likely than men to work in a legal profession early on in their career, and then withdraw to pursue family interests. Second, as the higher proportion of women graduating from law school has been a fairly recent trend, there are more younger than older female lawyers. Ninety-eight percent of the men in the various legal professions had undertaken or completed at least two years of postsecondary education, while only 81 percent of the women had, reflecting the fact that more men than women in the legal profession are lawyers, and therefore required to have completed at least two years of postsecondary education.

Should Canada, as a democratic society, aim for a 51 percent representation of women among lawyers, paralegals, and legal secretaries? This is a question that I hope readers will ponder carefully, because it has no easy answer. On the one hand, in a democracy there ought not to be discrimination against either men or women who aspire to become lawyers, paralegals, or legal secretaries. On the other hand, democracy values freedom of choice. Is the tendency of women to become paralegals and legal secretaries more frequently than men do the result of a free choice, or a hangover from a time when the options for women's careers were significantly more restricted than for men's? Or is it a bit of both? The report of a task force headed by former Supreme Court justice Bertha Wilson in 1993 showed that women in law firms often face significant barriers to their career advancement, ranging from overt sexism to more subtle obstacles such as the unwillingness of many firms to recognize the need for promoting a work-life balance so that family responsibilities can be accommodated. Wilson's report raised fundamental questions about how both male and female professionals can give due consideration both to their careers and to their families. These questions relate to issues of choice and equality of central importance to democracy, but they extend far beyond simple questions of representation. For many years, it has been the case that only half to two-thirds of those graduating from law school in Canada actually end up practising law. To be successful in practice, sacrifices often need to be made in other aspects of life, and many law school graduates who decide not to practise law - women and men - have sought employment in areas that allow more scope for family life.

ABORIGINAL PEOPLES

Aboriginal peoples are seriously underrepresented in the legal profession. In 1996, 2.6 percent of Canada's population identified with at least one Aboriginal group, and 3.7 percent reported at least one Aboriginal ancestor. But only 0.86 percent of legal professionals in Canada in the 1996 census year identified with an Aboriginal group, including 0.7 percent of Canadian lawyers and 1.3 percent of paralegals. In general, Aboriginal people in Canada tended to have high rates of unemployment, and accounted for only 1.9 percent of the experienced labour force in the census year.

Aboriginal legal professionals were at least as well educated as non-Aboriginal professionals in the same categories, but nevertheless earned

40 percent less than legal professionals as a whole, with Aboriginal lawyers earning 45 percent less. This difference in income is explained partly by the fact that on average, Aboriginal legal professionals are significantly younger than other legal professionals (four years younger among the lawyers), and therefore fewer have attained senior positions. In addition, a disproportionate number of Aboriginal people in the legal profession seek work outside of mainstream law firms and large cities, preferring to reside closer to Aboriginal communities where high-income employment opportunities are not as prevalent. And finally, barriers stemming from discrimination continue to exist.

VISIBLE MINORITIES

Nearly 11 percent of the Canadian population fifteen and over is made up of visible minorities, and they constitute 10 percent of the experienced Canadian labour force. Visible minorities also account for nearly 10 percent of paralegals, meaning that they are equitably represented in this group. As well, legal secretaries are close to equitable representation, with visible minorities making up 8 percent of this group. Only 4.5 percent of Canada's lawyers are visible minorities, however, which accounts for the fact that of those working in the legal professions in general, only 6.5 percent, or 20,570, were visible minorities in 1996. Underrepresentation of visible minorities among lawyers may be an indication of the difficulties faced by new immigrants in obtaining the funds required to attend law school. The rapidly increasing fees of law schools may well exacerbate this imbalance.

Visible minorities in the legal professions were, on average, three years younger than those in the legal professions overall, and tended to be slightly better educated. Like Aboriginal Canadians and women, however, they earned significantly less than most of their colleagues: only about 70 percent of the average income in the legal sector. This differential can be attributed to the relative youth of visible minorities in the legal professions, their underrepresentation among lawyers, and probably to some extent by discrimination.

Many visible minorities are also immigrants. This leads to the question, discussed below, of how well represented immigrants are in the legal professions.

IMMIGRANTS

In 1996 immigrants (defined as those who had at any time been landed immigrants) represented nearly 21 percent of the Canadian population aged fifteen and above, and 19 percent of those in the experienced labour force. Like visible minorities, the immigrant population is underrepresented among lawyers, constituting only 11.6 percent (6,845) of them. And like visible minorities, immigrants were better represented among the lower ranks of the legal professionals, making up 16.5 percent of the legal secretaries and 17 percent of the paralegals. In spite of this underrepresentation, it is encouraging that the proportion of immigrants in the legal profession increased dramatically between 1991 and 1995. Among lawyers, there was a 24 percent increase, and there was a 43 percent increase among paralegals and related occupations.

Unlike women, visible minorities, and Aboriginal peoples, immigrants tended to be a little older than other employees in the justice system, which is explained by the fact that immigrants in the experienced labour force tend to be a little older than nonimmigrants. They had roughly the same educational attainment as other members of the legal professions, but earned only about 86 percent of what the Canadian-born earned, due to the fact that they are overrepresented in the lower-paying sectors of the legal professions.

Judges

Given the underrepresentation of women, Aboriginal Canadians, visible minorities, and immigrants among lawyers, these groups are bound to be similarly underrepresented among judges.

There were 2,011 judges in Canada in 2001, nearly evenly divided between federal and provincial/territorial appointments, with 51 percent being federal appointments (Snowball 2002, 7). About 93 percent of the judges were trial judges, while the remaining judges served on an appellate court. Eighty-two percent of the judges worked full-time, while the remainder were "supernumerary" (partly retired judges working a reduced load). In 1996 the average salary of judges at all levels was $126,000 (Goudreau 2002, 8). In 2005 judges in the Federal Court of Canada earned $226,200 and in the superior courts across Canada $224,200 annually (Office of the Commissioner of Federal Judicial Affairs), while Supreme Court of Canada judges earned $266,800. Chief justices make slightly more. For example, the chief justice of Canada earned $288,200 in 2005. Judges appointed by the provincial governments tend to earn somewhat less than their federally appointed counterparts. In 2005 judges of the Ontario Court of Justice earned $213,630 annually.

Although not a great deal of research has been conducted on the backgrounds of Canadian judges in a historical sense, what evidence there is confirms that until the movement to reform the judicial appointment process began in the 1970s, the Canadian judiciary significantly overrepresented men of British and French origin and underrepresented women, new Canadians, Aboriginal Canadians, and visible minorities, especially in Ontario, Quebec, and the Atlantic provinces (McCormick and Greene 1990). The new appointment procedures have dramatically increased the proportion of women in the judiciary, as well as of visible minority judges, particularly in Ontario, and of Aboriginal judges, particularly in western Canada.

As well, the proportion of judges with significant partisan political experience has declined since the early 1970s. Although it is difficult to measure the number of judges who had been members or strong supporters of a political party before their appointment, the proportion has probably declined from more than 80 percent in the early 1970s to about 60 percent in the late 1990s (Greene et al. 1998, 36). This is not to imply that partisan political experience is necessarily an inappropriate background for a judge. Indeed, experience as a candidate, or going door-to-door with candidates during elections, can provide a very healthy dose of reality to those from privileged backgrounds who might otherwise have very little experience with the real problems of ordinary people. The system of judicial appointments that prevailed in Canada up to the 1960s, however, tended to limit judgeships to those with political experience, a factor that helped to mitigate against judicial selection based on merit alone.

GENDER

The proportion of women judges has steadily increased from less than 6 percent in 1990 to nearly 25 percent of full-time judges in 2001 (Snowball 2002; McCormick and Greene 1990). Outside of Quebec and British Columbia, which do not provide data on gender, 24 percent of the full-time judges were women, compared with only 4 percent of the supernumerary judges. (This is an indication that younger judges are more likely to be women than are the older, semi-retired judges.) The lower proportion of women judges relative to the proportion of women lawyers is understandable, given that judges are appointed until their retirement, and it will take some time for the predominantly male judiciary of the 1990s to be replaced by a judiciary more reflective of the gender balance in the legal profession.

Figure 3.1 shows the proportion of women judges in 2001 in the jurisdictions where data are available. The proportion of women judges varied considerably across the country. Outside of Nunavut, where one of the two trial court judges was female, the Supreme Court of Canada had the highest proportion of women judges – one-third – followed by Manitoba at 28 percent. Newfoundland and Yukon had the lowest proportions of women judges: 14 percent and zero, respectively. It should be noted that as of 2004, four of nine Supreme Court of Canada judges were women.

Whether the proportion of women judges will ever catch up with the proportion of women in the legal profession or the proportion of women in the population depends on a combination of the political will of the appointing authorities and the willingness of women to accept judgeships. The latter depends on how inviting the judicial work atmosphere is for women candidates. Justice Wilson's study of gender equality in the legal profession pointed out some of the disadvantages

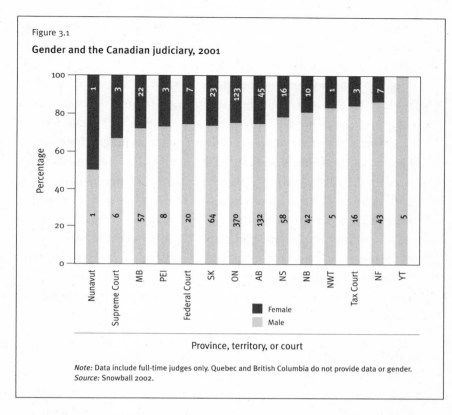

Figure 3.1

Gender and the Canadian judiciary, 2001

Note: Data include full-time judges only. Quebec and British Columbia do not provide data or gender.
Source: Snowball 2002.

that women judges face, from an absence of washroom facilities within reasonable walking distance to circuit schedules that make it impossible to accommodate family responsibilities (Wilson 1993). Wilson's biographer has demonstrated that her report has had an impact, and that many chief judges and justices now put more effort into accommodating the reasonable needs of women judges, meaning that women lawyers are more likely to apply for and to accept judgeships than before (Anderson 2001).

Will a higher proportion of women judges make a difference to the justice system? On the one hand, according to judicial positivists, an impartial application of the law will lead to the same results regardless of the gender or any other background characteristic of a good judge. But the "realist" view is, as its name suggests, a more accurate description of the judicial role. No matter how impartially a judge attempts to act, there are areas where judicial discretion is unavoid-able. As Wilson herself has argued, gender is not likely to make a dif-ference in judicial decision making in areas of the law where there is rarely a "uniquely feminine perspective," such as "the law of contract, the law of real property and the law applicable to corporations." Wilson identifies the criminal law, however, as an area where female judges sometimes have different perspectives from male judges, for example because of "presuppositions about the nature of women and women's sexuality" (Wilson 1990, 515). Women may have a different perspective both because of nature (a tendency to place issues in a broader per-spective) and nurture (women's unique experiences). She argues that a higher proportion of women judges will help to make the development of the law more "fully human" (p. 522). In addition, the presence of more women on the bench can serve as an example to encourage younger women to pursue careers in law with the real possibility of a judicial career.

ABORIGINAL JUDGES

According to the Manitoba Aboriginal Justice Implementation Commis-sion (Chartrand et al. 2001), in 2001 there were eighteen Aboriginal judges in Canada, representing 0.8 percent of the Canadian judiciary. Thus, the proportion of Aboriginal judges is about the same as the pro-portion of Aboriginal lawyers, but about a third of the overall propor-tion of Canadians who identify themselves as Aboriginal. The salaries of Aboriginal judges were on average 42 percent lower than the aver-age salary of judges in Canada (Goudreau 2002, 22), meaning that the great majority of Aboriginal judges have appointments at the inferior court level. In 1988 there were only two Aboriginal judges in Canada, and so a great deal of progress has been made since then to make the Canadian judiciary more representative of Aboriginal peoples.

Like the increased representation of women in the judiciary, having more Aboriginal judges will serve an educative function for non-Abo-riginal judges, and will have an impact on the development of the law. But the appointment of more Aboriginal judges is likely to have even more far-reaching effects. This is because many Aboriginal people think of the Canadian justice system much more as the instrument of a foreign occupying power than as their own justice system, one that they've had a hand in designing and running. For example, Aboriginal traditions tend to place more emphasis on restitution and rehabilitation than on proof of guilt, while the Anglo-Canadian system tends to take the opposite approach. The concept of "getting off on a technicality" has never been part of the Aboriginal approach to justice. From the Aboriginal perspective, the Canadian justice system often discourages responsibility and honesty. For example, the Inuktitut word invented by the Inuit for "lawyer" means "the one who lies for you," and the word for "prosecutor" means "the one who wants to send you to jail" (Dutil 1999, 433). As the number of Aboriginal judges increases, Aboriginal concepts of justice are also more likely to affect the nature of the Canadian justice system.

Aboriginal concepts such as sentencing circles are already becoming more commonplace in parts of Canada with a proportionately larger Aboriginal population, such as Manitoba, Saskatchewan, Nunavut, and the Northwest Territories. Sentencing circles involve members of the Aboriginal community in discussing with an offender the impact of the offence on victims, appropriate restitution, and appropriate treatment or punishment that is likely to lead to rehabilitation. They provide nonbinding advice to judges, and have been shown to have a positive social impact with regard to both rehabilitation and reconciliation in a number of instances (Lafond 1999; Dumont and Smith 1999). As well, since the late 1990s the RCMP has promoted restorative justice through programs such as the Community Justice Forums. These programs represent alternative measures that are intended to empower Aboriginal communities and to encourage offender responsibility and reconciliation between victims and offenders (Cooper 1999, 427). Jean-Luc Dutil (1999, 438), a judge with many years of experience in the Quebec Arctic, has noted a significant reduction in crime in general, and violent crime in particular, as a result of such restorative justice initiatives.

Visible Minority and Immigrant Judges

Little information is available about the proportion of visible minority judges in Canada, or about the proportion of judges who came to Canada as immigrants. There is a great deal of evidence, however, that visible minorities and new Canadians have traditionally been under-represented among Canadian judges, although this underrepresentation is likely not as severe as we enter the new century as it was twenty years earlier (McCormick and Greene 1990, 33; Russell 1987).

The underrepresentation of new Canadians and visible minorities is more pronounced in the appellate courts than the trial courts. According to a survey in the early 1990s, only about 6 percent of Canadian appellate court judges claimed to be members of one of the more recent ethnic groups to arrive in Canada, and only 5 percent were born outside Canada (compared with about 20 percent of the Canadian population). And visible minority judges earned 27 percent less than the judicial average in 1996, meaning that they tend to be appointed more often to the inferior courts than to the superior courts (Goudreau 2002, 26).

High Achievers

Canadian judges tend to be high academic achievers, and appellate judges tend to have the highest records of achievement. In addition to attaining the high level of academic achievement necessary to get accepted into law school, for example, 90 percent of appellate judges had received significant academic awards or honours. In the mid-1990s, 70 percent of Canadian appellate judges had completed a bachelor's degree (rather than the two years of undergraduate education mandatory for lawyers), 17 percent had completed a master's degree, and 9 percent had completed a doctoral degree. One-third had published academic articles or books, and one-quarter had received honorary degrees. When the family backgrounds of Canadian judges are examined, it is evident that most come from family situations conducive to the fostering of high achievers. For example, half of the appellate judges' fathers and a third of their mothers had been educated beyond high school.

Interestingly, half of Canadian appellate judges had relatives who were or had been judges (Greene et al. 1998, 34-6). It is human to want to emulate the careers of other family members, and this natural tendency is one reason the demographic characteristics of the judiciary tend to lag behind the changing demographics of the broader population.

Although the Canadian judiciary is becoming more representative of women, visible minorities, and Aboriginal Canadians, the judiciary is likely to continue to overrepresent the best-educated, highest-achieving portion of these groups. When the backgrounds of Canadian MPs and members of provincial legislatures are compared with those of judges, judges tend to be higher achievers. As merit continues to supplant political patronage as the most important criterion for judicial appointments, the proportion of high-achieving judges may well increase.

The fact that judges tend to be high achievers is not necessarily bad in the context of thinking about a representative judiciary. But high-achieving, highly educated judges may not have the same perspectives about important social policy issues as Canadians whose achievements and education are average, and so there might be a dissonance between the approach taken by judges, when they may legitimately apply their discretion, and the perspectives of Canadians as a whole. The contrast between judicial decisions supportive of making same-sex marriage available to promote equality, and the somewhat less supportive views of Canadians – particularly older Canadians in the same age bracket as the judges – may be a case in point (Mendelsohn 2003). Those who are more highly educated tend to be more supportive of minority rights, and more tolerant of difference (Sniderman 1975). As the new millennium progresses, such examples of dissonance between the judiciary and the public may result more from differences in education and achievement than in ethnicity, race, or gender.

Court Support Staff

It is important for court support staff to be representative of Canadian society for two reasons. First, court staff represent the public face of the courts, the first contact point for litigants and witnesses. If litigants and witnesses do not see their own backgrounds represented in the courts, they may not view the court as an institution that is an integral part of their own cultural system. Second, all Canadians should feel that they have an equal opportunity to work in the courts should they so desire, and that they are not likely to encounter discrimination when applying for a court-related job.

Court support staff include administrative staff (court administrators, court clerks who are also justices of the peace, trial coordinators, and registrars), court reporters and transcriptionists, sheriffs and bailiffs (staff who serve writs and summonses, seize property, or enforce court orders), and court clerks who perform more minor administrative functions. Statistics Canada has provided some information about the backgrounds of these four groups, although the data are somewhat unreliable because they include some reporters (such as Hansard reporters) who work outside the courts, and because there is some overlap between the first and fourth categories. Nevertheless, these data do provide some indication of the extent to which court support staff are representative of Canadian society as a whole.

In 1996 some 14,125 persons were reported to have been working in these court support occupations, including nearly 4,000 administrative staff, over 5,500 reporters and transcriptionists, about 2,500 sheriffs and bailiffs, and about 2,700 court clerks (Goudreau 2002, 7). A more recent report, however, shows about 12,000 court support staff in 2001 on federal and provincial payrolls (Snowball 2002, 10). The difference could result from the fact that many court reporters and transcriptionists were self-employed, providing services to the courts on a contract basis.

GENDER

Two-thirds of the court support staff were women, and they tended to be a few years younger than their male counterparts. Women accounted for 61 percent of the administrative staff, 81 percent of the clerks, and 93 percent of the reporters and transcriptionists. Nearly all of the sheriffs and bailiffs, however, were men. Within each of the court support staff categories, women tended to earn significantly less than men. Among the administrative staff, the average salary of women was about $39,000, as compared with $51,000 for the men. Women reporters and transcriptionists earned on average about $30,000, compared with nearly $43,000 for the men. And the male sheriffs and bailiffs earned about $38,000, compared with $30,000 for the women (Goudreau 2002, 18). The fact that the women employees tended to be younger explains only part of the salary differential.

ABORIGINAL PEOPLES

About 2 percent of court support staff in 1996 were Aboriginal Canadians, in large measure thanks to the success of programs designed to recruit and train Aboriginal Canadians to work in the courts. Court support services are now much closer to being representative of Aboriginal Canadians than the judiciary. The employment of a significant number of Aboriginal people in court support positions is a recent phenomenon, however, so that Aboriginal court support staff tended to be about five years younger, on average, than their counterparts, and as a result tended to earn less ($40,000 as compared with $51,000 for all court services personnel), and to work part-time more often than court personnel in general. Nevertheless, 77 percent of the Aboriginal people working in the courts had two years or more of postsecondary education, compared with 74 percent of court personnel in general, which is a positive sign for future promotions for Aboriginal employees (Goudreau 2002, 20).

Interestingly, Aboriginal Canadians represent about 3 percent of Canada's police forces, meaning that the police are now representative of Canada's Aboriginal population. Cleve Cooper (1999) has written about how the RCMP has made serious efforts to include more Aboriginal peoples in the force through a number of programs. For example, between 1995 and 1998, there were 207 graduates from the Aboriginal Cadet Development Program, and by 1998 there was a 5 percent participation rate of Aboriginal members in the RCMP (423). A number of reserves have also set up official or unofficial Aboriginal police forces.

VISIBLE MINORITIES

Visible minorities constituted about 6 percent of court support staff in 1996, compared with about 10 percent of the labour force. Thus, visible minorities are better represented among court support staff than among lawyers, but less well represented than among paralegals and legal secretaries. Efforts to promote employment equity for visible minorities among court support staff appear to have been less successful than for Aboriginal Canadians. Visible minorities working in the courts were significantly better educated than court support staff in general (86 percent had completed at least two years of postsecondary education, as compared with 74 percent of court personnel overall), tended to be about three years younger, and earned about 80 percent of the average earnings of court personnel (Goudreau 2002, 24-5).

IMMIGRANTS

Immigrants accounted for about 14 percent of court support staff, compared with their 19 percent participation in the Canadian labour force. They tended to be slightly older than other court support staff and had about the same amount of education, but tended to earn somewhat less (Goudreau 2002, 27-9).

Litigants

Up to this point, we have looked at the representative nature of Canada's courts from the perspective of court personnel. The other side of the coin is the litigants – those who appear in court as a result of a criminal charge, or as a result of a civil suit brought by themselves or an opponent.

Although there is not a great deal of information available about the backgrounds of civil litigants, anyone who spends time in courtrooms hearing private law cases can see that the majority of litigants in the civil courts are fairly well off. Large corporations are not infrequent litigators. The exceptions are the small claims cases. Given the small proportion of small claims judges compared with the substantially greater number of non-small-claims trial judges on the civil side, it is clear that the civil courts devote more resources to wealthy litigants.

On the criminal side, just the opposite is the case. The majority of criminal accused persons hail from the ranks of Canadians of lower socioeconomic status, and visible minorities and Aboriginal Canadians are significantly overrepresented. The majority of criminal cases are heard at the inferior court level, while the majority of private law cases are heard by a superior court judge. This is because one of the basic principles of the anglo-Canadian justice system has always been to have inferior courts handle "routine cases with less serious possible outcomes" (McCormick 1994, 23). Peter Russell (1987) has drawn attention to this imbalance and questioned whether in a democracy it is acceptable to allocate "superior" judges mostly to the rich, and "inferior" judges mostly to the poor. The solution, from his perspective, would be a unified trial court, with one level of judge for the rich and the poor.

The contrast between the superior and inferior courts has become even greater as a result of cuts to legal aid budgets across the country of around 25 percent between 1994 and 1997. Figure 3.2 shows provincial and federal government expenditures on legal aid up to 2001. In the mid-1990s, cash-strapped provincial governments began to slash their legal aid funds, which resulted in a significant increase in the proportion of self-represented litigants (SRLs) in court. By 1997 in Ontario, for example, no legal aid was available to a single person with an annual income over $15,000, or to a person in a family of seven with a family income over $40,000 (Statistics Canada 2001). A study conducted by the Department of Justice in Nova Scotia has shown that about half of SRLs would have preferred to have legal representation, had they been able to afford it (Nova Scotia 2004, 28). Because the inferior courts have a higher proportion of poor litigants than the superior courts, the cuts to the legal aid budgets have had a disproportionate impact on the litigants in the inferior courts.

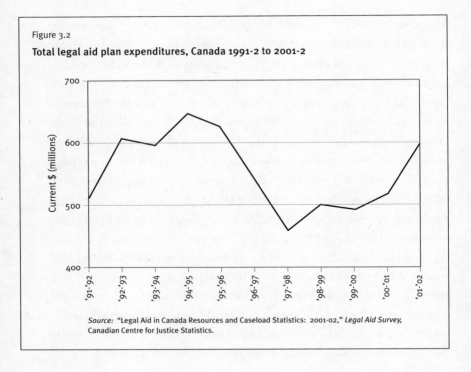

Figure 3.2

Total legal aid plan expenditures, Canada 1991-2 to 2001-2

Source: "Legal Aid in Canada Resources and Caseload Statistics: 2001-02," *Legal Aid Survey,* Canadian Centre for Justice Statistics.

The Nova Scotia study also shows, however, that nearly half of the self-represented litigants would not have hired a lawyer even if they could have afforded to do so. A look at the education levels and ages of SRLs may indicate why so many choose not to hire a lawyer. More than two-thirds have at least some postsecondary education at a university or community college. A quarter have a community college diploma, 10 percent have a bachelor's degree, and 7 percent have a graduate degree. As well, 70 percent are less than forty-five years old – not at the top of their earning potential. In fact, nearly two-thirds of the SRLs earned less than $30,000 annually. Being fairly well educated but without a great deal of income, a number of litigants reported that under the circumstances, they felt competent enough to represent themselves. Of the two-fifths of SRLs who clearly did not want a lawyer, one-fifth said their issue was so simple that a lawyer was not required, another fifth reported that they could do as good a job themselves, and one-sixth had had a previous bad experience with a lawyer; the rest gave a variety of different reasons. For example, I know an MBA graduate in her early thirties who opted to do the legal work herself to probate a family member's estate because she thought she could do a better job of ensuring that her late relative's wishes were carried out than a lawyer who had never met the deceased. She followed instructions in the literature now readily available for SRLs, finding the process time consuming but not difficult, and she saved about $10,000 in legal fees.

The Nova Scotia study showed that half of the cases with SRLs involved family matters, one-fifth involved debt recovery or personal injury, and one-eighth concerned criminal issues. Half of the SRLs reported obtaining the information they needed for their litigation primarily through the Internet, while two-fifths reported relying primarily on court staff. At a conference of Canadian court administrators that I attended in 2004, court staff from across Canada commented on the strain and workload created by the dramatic increase in the number of SRLs in recent years. While court staff try to provide as much information as they can about court procedures and how to fill out the appropriate court documents, they must be very careful, as impartial administrators, not to provide the kind of legal advice that is the purview of lawyers or paralegals. Many found it difficult to decide where to draw the line, and SRLs are sometimes frustrated that they cannot obtain more information from court officials. In order to meet the demand for information for self-represented litigants, courts have responded with pamphlets, videos, and interactive web-based resources on procedures in various kinds of cases. As well, legal information societies affiliated with provincial law societies have published books and pamphlets, sponsored workshops, and opened telephone help lines. Various publishing houses have also produced self-counsel books to assist litigants in such areas as drawing up and probating wills, incorporating, and divorce.

Given the large number of cases involving SRLs and family law, another issue is how the courts can deal appropriately with family relationship problems, which are often highly emotionally charged, without the assistance of lawyers. Lawyers can often take the emotional edge off litigation because they are not personally involved in fights over such issues as property and child custody. When a self-represented litigant, for example, is cross-examining a former spouse, it becomes more difficult to ensure that questions are appropriate and respectful. New strategies are required by judges and court staff so that legal issues are handled suitably.

Before the age of legal aid, judges sometimes appointed lawyers to represent SRLs who needed assistance. Typically, the judge would direct one of the other lawyers in his or her courtroom to represent the SRL, and the lawyer would feel obliged to do so by virtue of being an "officer of the court." All lawyers are designated as officers of the court, meaning that they have a duty to be truthful, and to assist the court when asked to do so. This is one way in which a lawyer could support the community by providing some pro bono (unpaid) legal services. Before legal aid, doing a certain amount of pro bono work was considered one of the obligations of being a member of a privileged and honourable profession. Although legal aid has been greatly beneficial to society in ensuring that poverty does not stand in the way of legal representation, and in providing the poor with more systematic access to legal representation than the informal pro bono system did, it is difficult to devise a fair way of limiting the cost of legal aid, particularly during economic downturns.

Community legal clinics in Canada have proven to be an effective and cost-conscious way of ensuring that legal advice is available to those who can least afford it. Lawyers in these clinics are usually dedicated to their work and expert in the kinds of issues they deal with (for example, landlord and tenant disputes, immigration issues, and some family matters). Community legal clinics might also represent an effective way of providing high-quality legal representation, at a reasonable cost to the public, to criminal defendants who cannot afford private lawyers. The establishment of such "public defender" systems, however, is usually opposed by the private bar. Private lawyers often claim that public defender systems are likely to provide inferior representation (as is apparently the case in some US jurisdictions), and there is no doubt that they will have an impact on the income of lawyers in private practice. According to judges that I have interviewed over the years, however, lawyers in private practice are sometimes inexperienced in dealing with certain kinds of criminal issues, while the lawyers at community legal clinics develop an expertise in the areas of law in which their clients are commonly involved.

If we assume that representation by a lawyer often results in fairer results, the increase in unrepresented litigants surely results in a justice system that is, on balance, less fair to the poor. In August 2003 Chief Justice Beverley McLachlin drew attention not only to the unfairness caused by the increasing number of unrepresented litigants, but also to the increasing delays that result from the longer time it takes for SRLs to pursue their cases. (Lawyers are usually skilled at getting to the important legal issues more quickly.) "I don't mean to suggest that our institutions are in jeopardy or that the building is on fire," she said. "But at this juncture, we might have to do a bit more than changing the batteries in the smoke detectors" (Makin 2003). Part of the chief justice's concern might have stemmed from the fact that even in the Supreme Court of Canada, in recent years about one-sixth of leave to appeal applications have been filed by SRLs.

The challenge to the courts presented by cuts to legal aid and the burgeoning number of SRLs is complex. More public money for legal aid will not resolve the issue, given that so many people now want to represent themselves in their legal proceedings. The new challenge is to ensure that appropriate information is available to assist people in representing themselves, and that SRLS are accommodated appropriately by court staff and judges. For centuries, court processes have evolved taking into account primarily the perspectives of judges and lawyers. The increasing frequency of cases involving SRLs – a trend that is unlikely to diminish even if more money could be pumped into legal aid – demands a rethinking of these processes to give greater weight to the needs of litigants without lawyers.

How Inclusive Are Canada's Courts?

Are judges and court support staff - the people who often give the courts a "human face" - representative of Canadian society? The evidence is that Canada's courts, which were for so long the preserve of men of the leading families of the British and French settler communities, are finally becoming more representative of women, Aboriginal Canadians, visible minorities, and new Canadians. If these trends continue, the legal profession, the judiciary, and court support staff may fairly accurately reflect the reality of the Canadian demographic situation by about 2025. A legal community that is more accessible to the "have-nots" in society is more likely to promote an equitable distribution of wealth and justice than a legal community made up predominantly of the "haves" (Galanter 1974).

On the other hand, the judiciary and the legal profession may become even more the preserve of the high achievers, and high achievers tend to hail from socially and economically advantaged backgrounds. High achievers may also demand even higher salaries, putting a greater strain on society, and particularly on the poor, to pay for their services. As well, increasing frequency of self-represented litigants in court is necessitating the rethinking of traditional approaches to court administration. All this suggests a need for greater lay involvement in court administration and judicial selection so that the perspectives of Canadians who are disadvantaged either by their circumstances, or by their lack of a legal education, will be more likely to be considered in decisions about the administration of justice.

CHAPTER 3

Strengths

- Systemic barriers to employment in powerful positions in the courts, which have traditionally been faced by women, visible minorities, Aboriginal Canadians, and new Canadians, are being dismantled.

- Many Canadian law schools now have roughly equal numbers of men and women students.

- Some law schools have programs to encourage members of nontraditional groups to apply to law school and to help them succeed.

- Affirmative action programs to encourage Aboriginal people to become lawyers and court workers have been successful, although Aboriginal people are still the most underrepresented demographic group among those who work in the justice system.

Weaknesses

- Women still tend to predominate in the lowest-paying and lowest-status sectors of the courts: paralegals, legal secretaries, and court reporters.

- Women, visible minorities, immigrants, and Aboriginal Canadians who work in the justice system tend to earn less than their counterparts from more established groups.

- Although some law firms have work-life balance programs, lawyers with children find it challenging to devote adequate time both to parenting and to work in order to achieve promotions in the firm.

- Although those who work in the courts reflect the demographic diversity of Canadian society more accurately than ever before, the educational divide between judges, lawyers, and court staff and the rest of society may be increasing.

4

RESPONSIVENESS OF COURTS TO EXPECTATIONS: INDEPENDENCE, BEHAVIOUR, AND ADMINISTRATION

Canadians expect their judges to decide cases as impartially as possible. As well, judges are expected to behave judicially; if they do not, there must be appropriate remedies. And the courts themselves are expected to be responsive to the public demand for expeditious justice and respectful treatment of litigants and witnesses.

The primary purpose of courts is to resolve the disputes that come to them as impartially as possible according to the law. Probably the most important mechanism developed by our political system to promote judicial impartiality is judicial independence. The test for judicial independence is the degree to which judges feel they can decide impartially, without undue influence from outside the courtroom.

Judicial Impartiality and Independence

A central ingredient in a rule of law system is an impartial and independent judiciary. Absolute impartiality is impossible, but encouraging judges to decide as impartially as humanly possible is a goal worth striving for. We provide judges with as much independence as practically possible from the other branches of government and from other potential sources of undue influence so that they can be in a position to make impartial judgments. Any attempts to influence a judge's decision outside of the rules of the courtroom constitute violations of judicial independence, whether these attempts originate from elected politicians, public servants, private interests, or other judges.

Illicit attempts to influence judges might be direct, such as the bribes that were frequently offered to judges in England until the seventeenth century, threats to the safety of judges who don't toe the government line (such as was the practice of the Mugabe government in Zimbabwe in 2002), or a telephone call to a judge from a cabinet minister on behalf of a constituent. In 1976 it was revealed that three Canadian cabinet ministers, including Indian Affairs Minister Jean Chrétien, had telephoned or visited judges in an attempt to influence the outcome or the timing of judicial decisions (Russell 1987, 78-9). Following these revelations, Prime Minister Pierre Trudeau issued guidelines to his ministers that prohibited them from contacting judges about any case before the courts. Direct violations of judicial independence always involve clear attempts to pressure a particular judge to decide a case in a certain way or at a particular time.

Indirect breaches of judicial independence involve actions that are calculated to encourage a group of judges to decide certain kinds of cases in a particular way. These actions might take the form of salary reductions or erosion of the working conditions of impolitic judges (for example, those who fail to convict members of opposition parties on trumped-up charges), retaliations not uncommon in England before the eighteenth century. They might involve exploitation of the administrative arrangements or structures of courts with the intention of swaying judicial decisions, such as the 1979 attempt of an administrative official in British Columbia to relocate a judge who was about to declare a new provincial law unconstitutional (Russell 1987, 77-8). Imprudent practices by interest groups, politicians, or the media might also threaten judicial independence. For example, a newspaper might launch a campaign against provincial court judges for not imposing lengthy enough sentences on young offenders. Or an interest group advocating a particular policy outcome might organize a demonstration in front of the Supreme Court of Canada while the Court is hearing a case of consequence to the group. Or a cabinet minister might publicly criticize judges for not being tough enough on crime, as Conservative attorneys general in Alberta, Manitoba, and Ontario did during the 1990s.

In the early 1980s, Peter McCormick and I interviewed 130 judges at all levels in Ontario and Alberta. We asked all of them whether they perceived any threats to judicial independence. None perceived any threats to their independence at the time (McCormick and Greene 1990). A few, however, referred to the 1976 telephone calls mentioned above as indicative of the potential vulnerability of judicial independence. In stark contrast, in the mid-1990s, when my colleagues and I interviewed 101 of Canada's 125 appellate court judges, two-thirds of the judges thought that there were serious threats to judicial independence. Their concerns centred on a number of issues, including what the judges considered to be unwarranted pressure from special interest groups, irresponsible media reporting of judicial decisions, pressure to decide in a politically correct manner, open criticism of judicial decisions from some provincial attorneys general, lack of appropriate administrative support, and inappropriate procedures for determining judicial salaries (Greene et al. 1998). We were alarmed by this finding. Given the results of the earlier study, we asked whether the safeguards for judicial independence in Canada had begun to erode. An understanding of the historical development of the principle of judicial independence will put the recent concerns raised by appeal judges into perspective.

DEVELOPMENT OF JUDICIAL INDEPENDENCE IN ENGLAND

Judicial independence evolved in England along with the struggle for the rule of law, which itself can be seen as part of the evolution toward democratic government. The victors of the Glorious Revolution in 1688 had fought for the supremacy of Parliament and its laws over arbitrary decrees by the monarch, and they also demanded an independent judiciary to apply the law even-handedly (Plucknett 1940; Lederman 1956).

After 1688, the major theoretical defence of the idea of an independent judiciary was provided by liberal political theorist John Locke, who argued for "indifferent" judges to settle disputes about the application of the law so that the law would "not be varied in particular Cases, but [there should be] one Rule for the Rich and Poor, for the Favourite at Court, and the Country Man at Plough" ([1690] 1980, 75). For Locke, it was particularly important that members of the government be subject to the equal application of the law, so that no one would be "a judge in his own case" (p. 12).

The two means, written into law (Act of Settlement, 1701), for protecting judicial independence were appointment of central superior court judges for life during good behaviour, and the setting of judicial salaries by Parliament rather than by the cabinet. Previously, judicial appointments had been at pleasure, meaning that the monarch could remove judges whose decisions he or she disagreed with. "During good behaviour" meant that judges could be removed only by a joint address of both houses of Parliament, and then only because of behaviour inappropriate for a judge (such as accepting a bribe, consistently failing to attend at court hearings, or a serious lapse in morals). The setting of salaries by Parliament was intended to prevent the executive from manipulating judicial salaries in order to influence judges' decisions.

THE AMERICAN REVOLUTION AND THE SEPARATION OF POWERS

Debates about how best to protect judicial independence in Canada often refer to developments south of the border, and so it is useful to understand the somewhat different approach of Americans to the protection of judicial independence.

The framers of the 1787 American constitution were influenced not only by the arguments of John Locke but also by the ideas of William Blackstone ([1769] 2001) and the Baron de Montesquieu ([1750] 1989). Blackstone noted the "separation of powers" that had developed between the judiciary and the other branches of government in England. Montesquieu attributed the apparent success of the English system of government in preserving liberty to the separation of governmental powers into the legislative, executive, and judicial branches so that each branch could act as a check on potential abuses of power by the other two.

The idea of the separation of powers was intriguing to the framers of the US constitution, and as a result they enshrined the "judicial power of the United States" in its Article III. Much of the article was copied from the judicial provisions in the Act of Settlement, but Article III also recognized the judiciary as equal in status to the other two branches of government, an important departure from the principle of parliamentary supremacy in the British system. The framers of the US constitution intended the three branches of government to act as a check on each other through the exercise of separate powers, but they also meant to enable each of the three branches to meddle in the affairs of the other branches a little, to perform a balancing function. Thus, it is not surprising that in the early 1900s, US judges spearheaded a movement for judicial control over court administration. The thinking was that if the judiciary is a separate branch of government, then the judiciary must control its own administration. Other constitutional experts, however, reasoned that the separation of powers implied that the executive should administer the courts as a check on the judiciary (Baar 1975).

Ultimately, the movement for judicial control triumphed in the US federal courts in 1939. In most state and local courts, however, court administration remained the responsibility of the executive. In federal and state jurisdictions where the judges control administration, there has not always been a higher standard in administrative procedures, and the judges have often had to struggle to obtain adequate funding from the legislature (Millar and Baar 1982).

Canadian Contributions to the Advancement of Judicial Independence

As in many other areas of constitutional politics, Canada has borrowed ideas about how to promote judicial impartiality from both the United Kingdom and the United States, and has also developed its own unique approaches designed to counteract the weaknesses of the others.

Development of Judicial Independence in Canada

By 1867, judicial independence for superior court judges was an established constitutional convention both in the United Kingdom and Canada, and this convention became the primary safeguard for judicial impartiality at the time of the country's birth. The preamble to the Constitution Act, 1867 states that the founding provinces of Canada desire to be federally united "with a Constitution similar in Principle to that of the United Kingdom," which can be taken to mean that Canada inherited all of the constitutional conventions developed in the United Kingdom, including judicial independence. But some safeguards for judicial independence also appeared in our written Constitution. Section 99 of the Constitution Act, 1867 provides for the appointment to retirement during good behaviour of superior court judges, and stipulates that only a joint address of Parliament can remove them. Section 100 states that the salaries of superior court judges must be set by Parliament, not by the executive. So in sections 99 and 100, we see the two mechanisms for protection of judicial independence first enshrined in the Act of Settlement.

Thanks to the constitutional and social status of superior court judges, and the general understanding of the convention of judicial independence held by political elites, the independence of superior court judges was unchallenged up to the 1970s, except for a handful of cases where attempts by provincial governments to reduce the jurisdiction of their superior courts were prevented by lawsuits (Friedland 1995). The picture was less rosy in the inferior courts. Ontario chief justice James McRuer's Royal Commission on Civil Rights (1968) was scathing in its criticism of the lack of protection of independence among provincially appointed judges, justices of the peace (JPs), and members of administrative tribunals. These judicial or quasi-judicial officials were frequently appointed for political reasons and without adequate educational backgrounds, and their incomes and reappointments were often dependent on the whims of government officials. This was a major affront to convention, according to McRuer, and also a violation of the right of citizens to the competent and impartial adjudication of disputes under the law. McRuer's report led to sweeping changes in appointment procedures, security of tenure, and security of salary among Ontario's inferior court judges, and similar changes followed in the rest of the country. As we enter the new century, however, serious problems remain due to inadequate safeguards of the competence, independence, and impartiality of JPs in some provinces, and of members of some administrative tribunals.

Justices of the peace are provincially appointed judicial officers who have a wide range of responsibilities. Their office has its roots in the English justice of the peace system dating from the fourteenth century, whereby upstanding citizens from local communities were appointed to conduct administrative tasks and preside over minor cases. Canadian JPs described as "nonpresiding" are empowered to process documents that initiate or mark the continuance of court proceedings, and they can sign certain kinds of search warrants. "Presiding" JPs direct hearings regarding municipal offences such as traffic tickets and bylaw infractions, and minor provincial offences such as traffic violations. As well, they often conduct bail hearings for persons charged with serious offences. Some JPs, especially those who are nonpresiding, are appointed from among the ranks of court clerks. A sizable number of JPs, however, are appointed by provincial attorneys general based on patronage considerations. Of the JPs who are court clerks or patronage appointments, very, very few are lawyers, and many do not possess more than a high school education. The potential abuses that may result from poorly qualified persons making important decisions about rights and obligations should concern Canadians.

There have been attempts to improve the JP system. In the late 1980s, Ontario's Liberal government set up a selection system based on merit, and began providing appropriate training for newly appointed JPs. That system, however, languished under subsequent governments. In the late 1990s, Alberta established minimum qualifications for presiding JPs - a law degree and five years of experience - and a nonpartisan appointments system. This reform was challenged in court by the non-lawyer JPs, but in 2003 the Supreme Court upheld the constitutionality of Alberta's reform (*Ell* v. *Alberta* 2003). This paves the way for other provinces to follow suit.

Administrative tribunals separate from courts were established by federal and provincial governments in the first half of the twentieth century to adjudicate disputes involving such matters as labour relations, municipal zoning disputes, workers' compensation, and environmental regulations. These tribunals often require specialized adjudicators with experience that most judges lack. For example, most judges do not have a background in labour relations, whereas most members of labour relations tribunals are lawyers who have practised labour law on behalf of either unions or employers. Canada has thousands of members of administrative tribunals at the federal and provincial level.

Neither the federal nor provincial governments, however, have developed a systematic approach to ensuring that tribunal members are qualified, are selected according to merit, and have the independence and impartiality required to fulfill their adjudicative functions. The great majority of tribunal members are selected because of patronage considerations, and they are appointed for terms (for example, three or five years). The renewal of their appointments often depends on whether the government that appointed them in the first place has changed – a situation that hardly inspires confidence in their impartiality. The question of the appropriate qualifications, appointment procedures, tenure, and independence of members of administrative tribunals is becoming a more frequent subject of litigation, and the reforms required to ensure that administrative tribunals more closely adhere to the democratic imperatives of the rule of law, competence, and impartiality may come about more through court decisions than legislative reforms (Jones and de Villars 2004).

JUDICIAL CONTROL OVER COURT ADMINISTRATION

The debate is still raging in Canadian courts about whether increased judicial control over court administration would result in better protection of judicial independence and more effective administration, or whether greater judicial involvement would have the opposite results.

In the 1970s, some Canadian judges became concerned that administrative changes initiated by the executive branch to tackle backlogs of cases could seriously erode judicial independence. In Ontario, attempts by provincial officials to manage case flow in a more systematic way were resisted by some judges as encroachments on judicial independence. In an attempt to accommodate these concerns, the government introduced legislation to transfer administrative control of the courts to a committee of judges. This legislation was abandoned when it became clear that most lawyers and court administrators, as well as many judges, thought that judicial control over court administration would be disastrous because most judges lack administrative training (Greene 1982).

Meanwhile, the judiciary in federally administered courts gained some administrative independence in 1977. The Supreme Court became a separate government agency, with the registrar – who became "subject to the direction of the Chief Justice" – as deputy head. The position of commissioner for federal judicial affairs was established to provide some distance between the Department of Justice and the Federal Court and later the Tax Court, and the commissioner was also given responsibility for salary and pension administration for all federally appointed judges.

Some judges saw the administrative independence of the federal court system in the United States as a model to emulate. The Canadian Judicial Council, Canadian Judicial Conference, and various provincial court judges' associations passed resolutions in favour of greater judicial control over court administration. As discussed in Chapter 2, the council requested the chief justice of Quebec's superior court, Jules Deschênes, to investigate these issues. In *Masters in their own house* he recommended that the administration of all Canadian courts should, over ten years, be placed under the control of judges so that the judiciary could both preserve its independence and have adequate power to address serious administrative issues (Deschênes 1981). Budgeting for the courts would be handled much like the budgeting for the independent commissioners that report to Parliament (e.g., the federal auditor general), whose budgets are scrutinized by legislative committees rather than a central agency under the control of cabinet prior to parliamentary approval. The Canadian Judicial Council was aware, however, that many judges thought that increased involvement in administration would compromise their independence by bringing them too close to executive and legislative functions of government. It advocated only that the judiciary be consulted about administrative matters.

In 1985 Ontario's reform-minded attorney general Ian Scott appointed appellate judge Thomas Zuber to consider administrative reforms to Ontario's courts. Among his many recommendations, Justice Zuber (1987) proposed the regionalization of court administration, the creation of courts management committees to administer court services in each region, and a provincewide Courts Management Committee. The government implemented these recommendations, but gave the committees advisory rather than management responsibilities, with the attorney general retaining total formal control over court administration. The management committees included chief judges and justices or associate chiefs, court administrators, lawyers, and lay persons.

In 1993 the provincial government signed a memorandum of understanding with the chief judge of the Ontario Court (Provincial Division), which provided the chief judge with an executive coordinator responsible to the chief to liaise with senior court services personnel regarding administrative issues. As well, the chief judge was given responsibility for drafting some parts of the court's budget, and for some human resource functions for court support staff. In the mid-1990s, the chief judge reported that this new system was working "much better than expected" (Friedland 1995, 187).

In Quebec, a major dispute developed between the judiciary and the provincial government in 1986 when the provincial government attempted to fire half of the superior court judges' secretaries, and most of their ushers. There was no prior consultation with the judges, as this was a general cost-cutting measure in which the government cut the budgets of all government departments by about 10 percent. Chief Justice Alan Gold launched a suit against the government, claiming that the cuts constituted a breach of judicial independence. An injunction was granted to prevent the firing of the court staff, and the hearing of the main issue was adjourned indefinitely. This situation forced the government to reach an out-of-court settlement with the judges in which some of the staff positions were restored, and an uneasy truce was reached. In 1990 the government offered to give the judges management responsibility for the staff reporting directly to them, but with no role in drafting budgets. The chief justice of the Court of Appeal accepted this arrangement, but the chiefs of the Superior Court and the provincial court rejected the offer because they considered it too limited. Legislation was introduced in 1993 to set up a council of chief judges and justices to administer Quebec's courts, but many judges objected that the scheme would give too much power to the chief judges and justices, thus creating a different kind of threat to individual judicial independence. Thus, this legislation was abandoned (Friedland 1995, 195).

In 1993 Martin Friedland, a senior law professor at the University of Toronto, was commissioned by the Canadian Judicial Council to report on issues related to judicial independence and accountability. His 1995 report recommended greater administrative independence for the judiciary, not only to protect judicial independence but also because professionals in the public sector tend to perform better if they enjoy optimal autonomy in their working conditions. He envisioned that in each province, a board of judicial management would be created to administer all courts within the province. This judge-controlled court services organization would operate as an independent government agency. The board, with about a dozen members, would include the chief justices of the court of appeal, the superior trial court, and the inferior trial court, and one regular judge from each of these courts. As well, it would include three lawyers nominated by lawyers' associations, and three or four lay members appointed by the government. The board's budget would be submitted to the attorney general, who would have responsibility for taking it through the approval process in the central agencies and the legislature (Friedland 1995, 218-24).

Friedland's recommendations have not yet led to any reforms. But alarm bells went off about the dangers of executive-dominance over court administration in 2002, when the British Columbia government announced the closure of a number of courthouses without any consultation with the judiciary, and with little apparent concern about the impact of the closures on cases already scheduled. In an astonishing development, the province's chief judge defied the government, supported by a large majority of the province's lawyers as well as popular sentiment. Subsequently, a meeting between the attorney general and the chief judge resulted in a jointly signed memorandum of agreement that guaranteed consultation with the judiciary before future changes to the budgets or administration of the courts.

In another recent development, in 2003 the Canadian Judicial Council commissioned a study to propose alternative practical models of court administration. The report, based on extensive consultation with the judiciary and court support staff, was completed in 2005, and contains the following key recommendations:

> There is significant support for a model of court administration based on limited autonomy for the judiciary within an overall budget for court administration set by the appropriate legislative authority. Support extends further to linking this limited autonomy to the use of an independent commission for the prevention and resolution of disputes related to the overall size of the budget allocated to the judiciary. There is also a need for a professional court administration with a chief executive officer responsible to the Chief Justice ... This report concludes that an optimal model of court administration would be one which provides the judiciary with autonomy to manage the core areas of court administration while ensuring (by the carefully considered use of an independent commission) that the authority of the political branches over resource allocation is not used arbitrarily (Baar et al. 2005, 3).

The tension between judicial independence and control of courts administration is likely to remain a prominent issue during the first part of the twenty-first century. It is clear that Canadians have failed to develop an acceptable overall strategy for courts administration, although the Models report may initiate a period of substantive reform. Effective court administration must protect judicial independence on the one hand, and on the other must facilitate appropriate administrative procedures, including meaningful public consultation, for resolving problems in courts that are sometimes badly clogged, and occasionally nearly dysfunctional.

THE CHARTER OF RIGHTS

Since the Charter of Rights came into effect in 1982, the development of jurisprudence about judicial independence has been rapid, thanks to section 11(d), which affirms the right to be tried for an offence by an independent and impartial tribunal. Charter decisions about judicial independence have covered new ground, and have made an important contribution to the international debate about the scope of judicial independence.

Shortly after the Charter of Rights came into effect, lawyers for Walter Valente, who had been charged with dangerous driving in Ontario, mounted a defence based on the claim that provincially appointed judges are not independent, as required by section 11(d). As noted above, the independence of superior court judges is specifically guaranteed in the Constitution, but the independence of provincial court judges is protected only by constitutional convention. As a result, although provincial court judges have tenured appointments to retirement, they could be removed by the attorney general for behaviour deemed inappropriate for a judge. Their collective salaries are set by the cabinet rather than by legislation. Another point raised by Valente's lawyers was that the salary levels of provincial court judges are significantly lower than those of superior court judges, their working conditions are not as good, and they have less control over administrative matters than judges appointed by the federal government – all matters that some judges think weaken their independence.

The trial judge, a judge of the provincial court, sent the judicial independence question to the Ontario Court of Appeal to decide, and the case eventually landed in the Supreme Court of Canada. Meanwhile, several judges and JPs refused to hear cases until the issue was settled, a situation referred to by the media as the "judges' strike." The

Supreme Court declared that constitutional guarantees of judicial independence are not necessary as long as three "essential conditions" for judicial independence are adequately protected: security of tenure, financial security, and institutional independence. Security of tenure means that judges must be appointed during good behaviour, and – here's the new condition – can be removed only after a recommendation by an independent inquiry. Financial security means that the judges must have a legislated right to a salary that is high enough to discourage bribery. Institutional independence means judicial control over matters directly affecting adjudication, such as assignment of judges, sittings of the court, court lists, the allocation of courtrooms, and the direction of administrative staff carrying out these functions. The Court noted that the Canadian Judicial Council had not endorsed Chief Justice Deschênes's proposal that judges must have control over all aspects of court administration in order to protect their independence (*Valente* v. *The Queen* 1985).

The next case materialized, ironically, because of improvements that the federal government made to the pension benefits of superior court judges in 1975, which was the same year that Marc Beauregard was appointed to the Quebec Superior Court. Just after his appointment, Parliament created a compulsory contributory pension plan for superior court judges and increased their salaries, and the legislation was made retroactive to a date before Beauregard's appointment. Beauregard sued for violation of judicial independence, claiming that the government had tampered with his salary by forcing him to contribute to a pension plan that he had not been aware of. A decade later, when the case got to the Supreme Court, Chief Justice Brian Dickson, writing for the Court, declared that judicial independence has an individual aspect – to allow judges complete liberty to hear and decide the cases that come before them – and also a collective aspect. The collective aspect encompasses the independence required by the judiciary as an institution in order to provide impartial adjudication regarding all disputes about the law, including federalism and Charter cases. The collective aspect of "judicial independence means the preservation of the separateness and integrity of the judicial branch and a guarantee of its freedom from unwarranted intrusions by, or even intertwining with, the legislative and executive branches." The idea that collective independence needs as much protection as individual independence is an important contribution to thinking about judicial independence. Dickson concluded that because the pension legislation did not interfere either with individual judicial decision making, or collective independence, there was no violation of judicial independence (*Beauregard v. Canada* 1986, 77).

In a 1989 decision, *MacKeigan* v. *Hickman*, the Supreme Court ruled that judges cannot be forced to testify in court about how they decided particular cases. This case grew out of the murder conviction of Donald Marshall, Jr. in 1971. Two weeks after his conviction, several witnesses recanted their testimony, but this information was not relayed to Marshall's lawyer. In 1982, the Nova Scotia Court of Appeal reviewed the case, found Marshall innocent, and ordered him freed. Nevertheless, the court concluded that because Marshall lied in parts of his testimony in 1971, "any miscarriage of justice is more apparent than real." On their own, these remarks are clearly inappropriate. One of the judges on that appeal panel, however, had been Nova Scotia's attorney general in 1971, when the decision was made not to reveal the new evidence that cast doubt on Marshall's conviction. The furor that ensued led to a royal commission inquiry in 1986. The inquiry wanted the appeal judges to appear before it to answer questions about how the former attorney general had ended up on the panel, and what evidence the judges had used to blame Marshall. The judges refused to appear on judicial independence grounds, which led to litigation in the Supreme Court. The Court's unanimous decision was that judges cannot be forced to testify about the reasons for their decisions by an executive-created inquiry. But Justices Cory and Wilson dissented on the issue of whether judges could be compelled to testify about administrative issues such as how panels are struck, and even the majority concluded that judges did not have absolute immunity from answering questions about administrative matters before a properly constituted judicial council. This case may foreshadow the litigation we might see in the future if judges become more directly involved in administering the courts.

Perhaps the most far-reaching decision of the Supreme Court regarding judicial independence was the 1997 *Reference re Remuneration of Judges of the Provincial Court*. Several provincial governments had attempted to reduce the salaries of provincially appointed judges as part of an overall salary reduction in the public sector in the mid-1990s. Judges in Prince Edward Island, Manitoba, and Alberta objected to the way in which the salary cuts were instituted. Some judges saw the cuts as punishment for not making decisions more to the liking of their provincial governments. The judges' associations in these provinces initiated legal action, leading to a reference that ended up at the Supreme Court. The Supreme Court declared that to protect judicial independence, governments may not negotiate directly with judges' associations about salary and pension issues. Rather, governments must establish judicial compensation commissions (JCCs) – independent bodies that make recommendations about appropriate adjustments to judicial salaries at least every three years. Although the JCC recommendations are not mandatory, governments must give them "serious consideration," and the judiciary itself decides on the reasonableness of the government's response. In effect, this makes the judges the final arbiters of their own remuneration – a privilege enjoyed by no other public official.

The Supreme Court based its decision both on what the judges considered to be the implications of section 11(d) of the Charter, and on the convention of judicial independence. No matter how you read section 11(d), however, it is hard to conclude that the plain wording of this section mandates the existence of JCCs. As well, prior to this decision, no one ever suggested that the convention of judicial independence included JCCs. JCCs are an invention of the late twentieth century, not a time-honoured constitutional tradition. The creation of these arms-length bodies as a buffer between governments and judiciaries is, without a doubt, a good idea, and represents another important Canadian contribution to the theory and practice of judicial independence. But for the judiciary to state that JCCs are required by the Constitution not only underlines the potential scope of judicial discretion but also illustrates its potential for abuse.

Subsequent to the Supreme Court decision, a judicial compensation commission in Ontario recommended an increase in the annual salaries of provincial court judges from $110,000 to $170,000. The provincial government rejected the recommendation and was taken to court by the judges' association. The government's argument that its policy was to hold all salary increases to 2 percent did not convince the court that the JCC's recommendation had received serious consideration, and in the end the government granted the salary increase. In 2005, however, the Supreme Court upheld a decision of the Alberta government to reject a recommendation of the province's JCC for justices of the peace, noting that in order for a government to show that it has given serious consideration to the recommendations of the JCC, it must simply present "reasons that are complete and that deal with the commission's recommendations in a meaningful way" (*Bodner* v. *Alberta* 2005, 9).

THE FUTURE OF JUDICIAL INDEPENDENCE

The most important function of courts in a democracy is to provide an impartial forum for dispute resolution according to the law. The great majority of Canadians perceive Canadian judges to be impartial, in large measure because of their independence. The Constitution contains standard liberal-democratic provisions to protect the salaries and tenure of superior court judges to safeguard that independence. Decisions made under the Charter of Rights about judicial independence have substantially extended the constitutional guarantees. The *Valente* decision affirmed not only that provincially appointed judges must have security of tenure and minimal protection of salaries to protect independence. It also held that before a judge of the superior or inferior court can be removed from office, an impartial inquiry must recommend the removal. As well, the decision stipulated that judges must control those aspects of court administration that directly affect decision making. The *Beauregard* decision affirmed the collective as well as the individual aspect of judicial independence, and in 1997 the Supreme Court decreed that arms-length judicial compensation commissions are required to recommend judicial salaries. And although the

MacKeigan v. *Hickman* decision affirmed that judges cannot be required to testify about the legal decisions they've made, the decision implied that judges can be held accountable for their administrative decisions – an important point if judges are delegated greater administrative responsibilities.

In spite of the high standards for judicial independence that have evolved in Canada, problems remain when it comes to justices of the peace and members of administrative tribunals. A number of these important officials may not have the qualifications needed to decide competently, and many do not have the degree of independence needed to make impartial decisions (Doob, Baranek, and Addario 1991; *Ell* v. *Alberta* 2003).

One of the challenges currently facing the courts is whether judges should assume greater responsibility for court administration in order to protect judicial independence, or whether greater administrative involvement on the part of the judiciary might actually pose a greater threat to judicial independence. Greater judicial involvement means that more effective systems of caseflow management can be established, because only judges can make administrative decisions that directly affect adjudication. On the other hand, greater judicial involvement could leave judges vulnerable to political pressure to decide cases in a particular way in order to get a decent budget allocation from the legislature. The recommendation of the Models study to create an independent commission to prevent or resolve these kinds of disputes is innovative, however, and might just be the key to positive reform of court administration in Canada.

Judicial Discipline

A review of some of the leading cases involving the discipline of judges shows how difficult it can be to strike the right balance between allowing judges to speak out publicly on important issues affecting justice, and encouraging them to refrain from comments that could cause us to question their impartiality.

DISCIPLINE OF FEDERALLY APPOINTED JUDGES

Before 1971, those with complaints about superior court judges had to take them to the federal minister of justice. If a complaint had merit, the minister could initiate proceedings for a joint address of the Senate and House to remove the judge. The only time that a superior court judge came close to being removed was during the 1960s, after a royal commission inquiry was set up to investigate certain actions of Mr. Justice Leo Landreville prior to his judicial appointment, when he was mayor of Sudbury. There were rumours that he had used his public office for personal gain. The inquiry found that Landreville's prior behaviour had not been up to the standard expected of a judge, and Justice Minister Pierre Trudeau started the ball rolling toward a joint address of Parliament to remove him. Landreville resigned before he was removed, but in 1973 he obtained a declaration from the Federal Court that the commissioner of the inquiry had failed to act judicially and had exceeded his jurisdiction (*Landreville* v. *The Queen* [1974]; Russell 1987, 176-7; Friedland 1995, 82-90). Dissatisfaction with the way in which the Landreville issue had been handled led to the creation of the Canadian Judicial Council in 1971.

Until the late twentieth century, every province except Quebec had county or district courts, which were inferior courts presided over by federally appointed judges. These courts had a permanent presence in smaller cities, and in many situations litigants could choose whether to have a trial before a county or district court judge relatively quickly, or wait for a superior court judge on circuit. By the 1990s, all of these courts had been merged with the superior courts, but when they existed, four county or district court judges were removed through joint address of the Senate and House of Commons. The most interesting case was that of Manitoba judge Louis St. George Stubbs, who during the Great Depression converted to socialism. He published pamphlets that were openly critical of what he considered to be the biased decisions of superior court judges in favour of the rich, and he once held a meeting in a theatre to denounce the Manitoba Court of Appeal. An inquiry appointed by the federal cabinet opined that Stubbs's attacks on the superior courts "did great harm to judicial institutions" and recommended his removal. He was duly removed, and went on to become a member of the Manitoba legislature – clearly a more appropriate forum for his message (McCormick and Greene 1990, 52-3).

Since 1971, the Canadian Judicial Council has acted as a tribunal to consider complaints about federally appointed judges. The thirty-plus-member council is composed of all of Canada's superior court chief justices and associate chief justices. As the new disciplinary role of the council became known, the annual number of complaints increased from a handful to 200 in 1995-6, and has since levelled off to about 170 per year (Canadian Judicial Council 2002).

Complaints are initially reviewed by the chair of the council's Judicial Conduct Committee. Many complaints allege that a particular judge's decision was wrong, and the complainant is informed that the appropriate remedy is an appeal. A little over half the time, the chair requests comments from the judge who is the subject of the complaint, and reviews the record of the hearing in question. In the great majority of cases, the evidence does not indicate inappropriate behaviour. Occasionally (once or twice a year at most), the chair finds that a complaint may have merit, and requests a panel of three or five judges to consider it. If such a panel decides that there is serious evidence of inappropriate judicial behaviour, it may recommend a full inquiry, or alternatively it may "express disapproval" of a judge's behaviour. The council is limited to recommending or not recommending removal from office, or expressing disapproval of certain behaviours. A wider range of intermediate sanctions is currently not available (in contrast, some provincial judicial councils may recommend a temporary suspension of a judge, a fine, or appropriate remedial therapy). If a complaint is received about a judge who is a member of the council itself, the council's bylaws require that it be reviewed by an outside counsel.

From the council's creation in 1971 to 2003, it has convened fewer than ten inquiries. In 1981 Mr. Justice Thomas Berger of the BC Supreme Court made some critical remarks about the 5 November constitutional compromise at a convocation address, and his comments were picked up by the national media. A judge of the Federal Court complained to the Canadian Judicial Council that Berger had violated judicial independence by criticizing government policy. (Part of the convention of judicial independence is that judges and politicians must refrain from publicly criticizing each other.) The council set up an inquiry that concluded Berger had violated judicial independence. Its final report merely stated that Berger had been "indiscreet," and that this indiscretion did not constitute grounds for his removal. Berger resigned anyway (Russell 1987, 85-9).

Because the royal commission that investigated the wrongful conviction of Donald Marshall, Jr. was critical of the comments of the appellate judges who wrote that Marshall was in large measure responsible for his wrongful conviction, the Nova Scotia attorney general asked the Canadian Judicial Council to investigate. The council established an inquiry that concluded the judges had made a legal error, but that this did not constitute grounds for dismissal.

In 1994 a third inquiry was established regarding a judge whom some considered too infirm to continue his judicial duties. The judge requested a judicial review in the trial division of the Federal Court about whether infirmity was a legitimate grounds for removal. The court affirmed the right of the council to recommend removal for infirmity, but the judge resigned before the inquiry could be completed.

An inquiry in 1996 concerned a complaint about inappropriate judicial remarks. During a sentencing procedure, Quebec Superior Court judge Jean Bienvenue remarked that women could "sink to depths to which even the vilest man could not," and that the Nazis killed Jews "in the gas chambers, without suffering." An investigating committee of the Canadian Judicial Council concluded that Bienvenue had failed to uphold expected standards of impartiality, and recommended his removal. The judge resigned before being removed.

In 1999 the minister of justice requested a council inquiry regarding whether Quebec justice Robert Flahiff, who had been convicted under the Narcotics Control Act, should be removed. An inquiry was established, and Justice Flahiff resigned before it could be completed.

In 2002 a Quebec Superior Court judge publicly took sides in a local dispute about the sale of municipal property. The prominent newspaper

Le Devoir printed Mr. Justice Bernard Flynn's views after he spoke to one of its journalists. The Quebec attorney general requested a council inquiry. The council declared that while the judge's comments were "inappropriate and unacceptable," they were not a serious enough breach of the norms of judicial behaviour to justify removal.

Also in 2002, Mr. Justice Jean-Guy Boilard of the Quebec Superior Court sharply criticized the work of two of the lawyers involved in a lengthy trial of seventeen members of the Hell's Angels biker gang. The lawyers challenged the judge's impartiality, and so he withdrew from the case. He had already heard from more than 100 witnesses in a jury trial that had consumed nearly $3 million from the public treasury. Another judge took over the proceedings but aborted the trial. The Quebec minister of justice, outraged at these events, asked the council to investigate Justice Boilard. An inquiry was struck that declared that Boilard's decision to withdraw was "improper" but held that this mistake did not warrant his removal. The full council, however, did not agree that Justice Boilard had erred.

Several high-profile requests for investigations by the council were dismissed for lack of prima facie evidence. For example, REAL Women, an organization of conservative-minded women, requested the council to investigate whether the remarks of Madam Justice Bertha Wilson at Osgoode Hall Law School in 1990 indicated a feminist bias that disqualified her from continuing to sit on the Court (Wilson 1990). The following year, REAL Women asked the council to investigate whether a speech by Madam Justice Beverly McLachlin, in which she criticized the male bias in abortion and prostitution laws, violated judicial impartiality. In neither case did the council set up an inquiry, ruling that the speeches represented a balanced analysis. In 1999 Alberta appellate court justice "Buzz" McClung wrote to the *National Post* to complain about Supreme Court justice Claire L'Heureux-Dubé's criticism of his opinion in a sexual assault appeal. In his decision, McClung had written that the sexual advances of the accused "were far less criminal than hormonal," and that they were simply "clumsy passes." L'Heureux-Dubé had countered that McClung's expressions were "plainly inappropriate in that context as they minimize the importance of the accused's conduct and the reality of sexual aggression against women." In his letter to the *Post,* McClung linked stances like L'Heureux-Dubé's to suicides of young men, but later apologized, claiming that he had not known about a suicide in L'Heureux-Dubé's family. Several groups complained to the council about McClung's letter to the *Post.* A panel of the council decided not to establish an inquiry, but nevertheless criticized McClung's remarks as "inappropriate" (Morton 2002, 201-5).

A sequel to the McClung affair occurred in December 1999 when F.L. Morton, a well-known right-wing academic critic of judicial activism, wrote a letter to the *National Post* criticizing several speeches by Justice L'Heureux-Dubé in which she urged judges to strike down laws that discriminate against gays and lesbians. Morton's point was that L'Heureux-Dubé had violated the Canadian Judicial Council ruling in the Berger case: judges must not speak out on politically controversial issues of great public importance. Morton's position was considered by BC chief justice Allan McEachern for the council. After reviewing the text of the speeches, he found a balanced analysis of the changing jurisprudence relating to equality. In his view, the comments that Morton complained about relied on a reporter's summary of the speeches. He emphasized the importance of judges making speeches at academic conferences (Morton 2002, 206-11).

In 2002 Mr. Justice William Marshall of the Newfoundland Court of Appeal, in a decision upholding the provincial government's decision to spread pay equity payments over a number of years, included a section criticizing the Supreme Court's interpretation of section 1 of the Charter (*Newfoundland Assn. of Public Employees* v. *R.* 2002). He claimed that the Court's approach left far too much room for judicial discretion. The other two judges on the panel signed on to Marshall's decision without reasons. The *Globe and Mail* covered the unanimous decision as an example of the debate on judicial activism versus judicial restraint. Newfoundland's chief justice, Clyde Wells, sent a letter to the *Globe* criticizing the reporting of the story. He noted that the two judges who concurred in the result had not indicated that they agreed with Justice Marshall's reasoning, and that therefore Marshall's criticism of the Supreme Court represented only his own position.

In response, former federal Conservative cabinet minister John Crosbie wrote to the *Globe* to lambaste Wells's letter as a violation of judicial independence. His argument was that judicial decisions must stand on their own with no judicial commentary to "explain" them, and that Wells's letter was inappropriate. Crosbie launched a complaint with the Canadian Judicial Council. A panel of the council was struck that, after consulting outside counsel, completely exonerated Wells. The panel wrote that while it is unusual for a chief justice to attempt to correct media mistakes, such action might be justified in extreme situations. As well, responding to an error in reporting a decision is not the same as entering into debate about a political issue.

It should be remembered that before becoming chief justice of Newfoundland and Labrador, Clyde Wells had been the Liberal premier of the province during the death of the Meech Lake Accord. In fact, his opposition to the accord was a major factor in its defeat. At that time, John Crosbie was a Newfoundland member of the federal cabinet that was trying to push through the accord. The wounds from that battle had apparently not healed. But aside from the drama of the two old foes squaring off again in spectacular style, this episode raises some important questions about the appropriateness of the council's disciplinary procedures. Justice Wells's letter to the *Globe* was unprecedented, and Crosbie's argument that it violated the traditional posture of judges not to comment outside the courtroom on their decisions or the decisions of other judges is compelling. That the council would brush aside Crosbie's complaint so easily raises the suspicion that the council was circling the wagons. As well, it gives some credibility to Morton's argument that the council seems to be applying different standards to those who are in the circle, such as council members Wells and McLachlin, and to those on the outside, such as Berger, a left-leaning judge.

The image of circling the wagons was not dispelled by the council's response to remarks by appointed 1997 Supreme Court justice Michel Bastarache in *Lawyers Weekly* in January 2001. Bastarache was quoted as saying that he disagreed with the expansive interpretation of the Charter by the Supreme Court in some criminal law cases, and of the

Aboriginal rights sections of the Constitution in some land claims cases. He said that he hoped to persuade the Court to "revisit" some of its decisions in these areas. The Ontario Criminal Lawyers' Association complained to the council about these comments. The chair of the council's Judicial Conduct Committee closed the file on the complaint after considering comments from Bastarache and Chief Justice McLachlin, although he cautioned Bastarache to "exercise restraint when speaking publicly" (Morton 2002, 178-9).

It is curious that between 1994 and 2003, all the inquiries struck by the Canadian Judicial Council have concerned Quebec judges. Patronage still plays a role in the appointment of superior court judges, and this old style of politics may be particularly evident in Quebec. The system of handling and investigating complaints about federally appointed judges appears to be working fairly well – certainly better than the system (or lack of system) before 1971. But a better system of appointments that ensured top-quality judges in the first place would be preferable to a good system of cleaning up in the wake of mediocre appointments.

DISCIPLINE OF PROVINCIALLY APPOINTED JUDGES

Provincial governments created provincial judicial councils beginning in the 1970s. They are usually composed of the provincially and federally appointed chief judges and justices, and sometimes include lay and bar representation. These councils usually serve a dual function: to screen applicants for provincial judgeships, and to consider complaints about provincially appointed judges. Unlike the Canadian Judicial Council, the provincial bodies can often recommend a reprimand or treatment, instead of removal.

Prior to the *Valente* decision, provincially appointed judges could be removed by order of the attorney general. It is not known how many magistrates and judges were removed this way, but certainly more than a handful were. Since the creation of the judicial councils, the records of their inquiries have been in the public domain.

For example, in 1993 Ontario provincial court judge Walter Hryciuk was accused of making rude and sexist remarks about women over a period of years. His behaviour became the focus of an inquiry ordered by the Ontario Judicial Council when a Crown attorney complained that the judge had tried to kiss her at a party. Hryciuk was suspended with pay while Madam Justice Jean MacFarland conducted the inquiry. She recommended Hryciuk's removal on the grounds that his comments and behaviour made it impossible for him to be seen as impartial toward female litigants or witnesses. Hryciuk filed for a judicial review of some of the procedures at the inquiry, and the legal wrangling that ensued lasted several years until his retirement. All the time, he remained suspended with pay.

In 2001 the Supreme Court upheld the decision of an inquiry in Quebec that Judge Richard Therrien should be removed from office. When Therrien had applied for a judicial appointment, he had lied about the fact that he had been convicted for protecting terrorists during the October Crisis of 1970, although he had since been pardoned. The Supreme Court ruled that the public demands a high standard of conduct from judges. Failing to mention a criminal conviction and pardon when applying for a judgeship did not meet that standard.

In a handful of cases, a judge has been charged and convicted of a criminal offence. Being convicted of a criminal offence is clearly a violation of "good behaviour," and in such situations an inquiry would certainly recommend removal. Seeing the writing on the wall, in most such cases the judge simply resigns. For example, David Ramsay of Prince George, BC, resigned his provincial court judgeship before pleading guilty in the spring of 2004 to sexually assaulting several girls aged twelve to sixteen. Observers agree that these crimes were the most serious ever committed by a sitting judge in Canada, and the sentence – seven years – is probably the longest received by a judge (Armstrong 2004).

EVALUATION OF JUDICIAL DISCIPLINE IN CANADA

R. MacGregor Dawson (1922), the pre-eminent student of Canadian government during the twentieth century, claimed that judges perform at the highest level when they have a level of autonomy in their daily work situations that is in addition to the independence needed to decide cases impartially. For Dawson, the benefits stemming from the lack of judicial accountability (encouragement of excellence) far outweigh the disadvantages resulting from the occasional lapse of good judgment. The system of judicial removal could always be used to correct the most egregious abuses of judicial power.

While there are clearly benefits associated with judicial autonomy, current democratic expectations relating to the benchmark of responsiveness call for a finer net to screen out judicial misbehaviour. The creation of the Canadian Judicial Council and the provincial judicial councils has certainly helped. Problems still exist, however. First, Canadians are still generally unaware of the disciplinary roles of the councils. Second, the councils are in the position of sitting in judgment upon members of their own group when under attack from the outside. Third, except in some of the provincial judicial councils, there is very little public participation in the system of judicial discipline. Judges will understandably be reluctant to cede any of their powers of self-regulation, but to give the discipline procedure more credibility, the involvement of lay persons in judicial discipline procedures is inevitable. For the moment we can nonetheless conclude that the current system of judicial discipline works tolerably well.

It makes sense to be concerned about having appropriate systems to not only handle complaints but also ensure that adequate adjudication is improved. To this end, a system of judicial performance evaluation needs to be put in place. Martin Friedland (1995) has advocated a system of judicial performance evaluations that would operate along the same lines as the evaluation of professors by students, which is similar to those used in several state court systems in the United States. After each hearing, counsel, litigants, and witnesses could complete an evaluation of how they were treated by the judge and by other court officials. Was the judge polite? Did the witnesses have the opportunity to tell the truth as they knew it? Did the litigants think they got a fair and impartial hearing? What improvements could be made? To protect judicial independence, the evaluation forms would be seen only by the judge being evaluated, unless the judge wished to share them with others for analysis and advice. To date, no Canadian courts have implemented a system of evaluations, although some Ontario courts have established evaluations for newly apppointed JPs. Given the natural human tendency to fear any kind of criticism, this is understandable. But since the courts are an essential institution in our democracy, this gap is inexcusable and unacceptable.

Treatment of Litigants and Witnesses, Access to Justice, and Expeditious Justice

The majority of Canadians hold judges in high esteem, and have a much higher level of trust in judges than in elected officials (Mancuso et al. 2006). As well, Statistics Canada reports that Canadians are generally satisfied with the attempts of the criminal courts to provide fair trials, with about 40 percent in a 1999 survey reporting that the courts do a "good" job in this area, and about 30 percent judging that they do an "average" job. Only 7 percent of recent immigrants, 9 percent of visible minorities, 11 percent of women, 13 percent of Canadians with low incomes, 13 percent of Aboriginal Canadians, and 14 percent of Canadians with disabilities considered that the criminal courts did a "poor" job of ensuring fairness.

The judgment of Canadians is not as sanguine about the ability of the courts to provide expeditious justice. About 40 percent of Canadians consider that the courts do a "poor" job of "providing justice quickly," including 48 percent of disabled Canadians, 42 percent of Aboriginal Canadians, 39 percent of women, 35 percent of Canadians with low incomes, 25 percent of visible minorities, and 12 percent of recent immigrants. Only about 15 percent consider that the courts do a "good" job of providing expeditious justice (Statistics Canada 1999). Moreover, a 1987 survey by the Department of Justice found that nearly 90 percent of Canadians agree that there is a need to make the justice system more "sensitive and compassionate," although two-thirds of Canadians feel that the system treats most people who come into contact with it with respect.

As noted in Chapter 2, the Canadian Charter of Rights and Freedoms guarantees the right of persons charged with an offence "to be tried within a reasonable time" (s. 11(b)). During the 1990s, Supreme Court decisions did not set clear standards for court performance to avoid unreasonable delays, and there are still seriously backlogged criminal courts in large urban centres. Are these backlogs a result of under-funding? From 1996 to 2001, total expenditures on courts, in constant dollars, increased 13 percent across Canada. Total per capita expenditures also increased, but this rise has not been uniform across the country. For example, in Ontario, constant dollar expenditures increased by 11 percent. British Columbia, meanwhile, saw a 1 percent decrease, and this was before the round of cuts brought in by the Campbell government in 2002. Alberta has fared the best, with a 32 percent increase, and Prince Edward Island the worst, with a 9 percent decrease (Statistics Canada 2001). Budget issues alone therefore cannot explain the current problem with caseload backlogs.

Although shortage of facilities, judges, or Crown attorneys is one cause of delay, by and large unnecessary delays are a result of defence counsel taking on too many cases, the inability of defence counsel and Crown counsel to work out expedited disclosure arrangements, wasted time in court requesting additional adjournments, and delay as a defence strategy (Greene 1983; Millar and Baar 1982). The justice system could eliminate these delays if forced to do so by appropriate accountability mechanisms. The development of such mechanisms will be a major challenge for the courts in the new century.

Like today, the 1970s was a time of increasing backlogs in the court system and experimentation with new administrative arrangements aimed at reducing delay. For example, in 1973 the Ontario Law Reform Commission recommended a professional management approach to court administration in order to deal with the increasing backlog of cases. This approach was to have been tried in a pilot project in a region west of Toronto in 1975, but was abandoned when several judges stated that taking case flow out of their hands would violate judicial independence. As a result, in 1976 the Ontario government tabled draft legislation to transfer responsibility for court administration to a judicial council. This plan was quietly abandoned because some judges objected to such an extensive role in administration, and some lawyers warned the government that few judges had any expertise in administration. Since that time, the criminal courts in Ontario have experimented with a variety of strategies, including "blitzes" on backlogs in the slowest courts with additional judges and prosecutors, and diversion of some kinds of cases out of the court system. Nevertheless, the backlog problem, particularly in Ontario's largest cities, has clearly not been resolved.

Delays in the civil courts tend to be even longer than those in the criminal courts across Canada (Greene et al. 1998). Experiments with mandatory mediation and case management, however, have significantly reduced delays in some Ontario civil courts since 1996. Case management means that judges become involved in monitoring the pace of litigation, something that many judges thought illegitimate until recent years because of the constraints of the adversary system. Deadlines are set for a reasonable flow of cases through the courts, and if certain cases are behind, counsel are contacted and sometimes required to appear before a judge or case management master to explain the delay.

Case management is likely to be an effective tool in reducing unnecessary delays, but it will not work unless the great majority of the legal profession cooperate. More counsel would probably be willing to tackle the delay problem if lawyers' codes of ethics clearly prohibited the use of unnecessary delay as a strategy to assist clients, and if unnecessary delays caused by lawyer incompetence or mismanagement were more amenable to discipline.

The Responsiveness of Courts to Institutional Expectations

Courts are expected to decide cases impartially, to have in place an appropriate system for disciplining judges who stray from appropriate behavioural norms, and to provide decisions as expeditiously as possible.

The great majority of Canadian judges, both federally and provincially appointed, appear to be doing their level best to decide impartially and to eliminate bias wherever possible. As well, the guarantees of their independence are enviable from the perspective of just about every other country in the world. Because judicial independence has always been a major concern of Canadian judges, the levels of judicial independence and impartiality may well be among the highest of any liberal democracy, and some leading Supreme Court decisions on judicial independence have made an important contribution to the international debate about the nature of judicial independence and how best to protect it.

Nevertheless, challenges remain. Although we have moved a great distance toward a merit-based system of appointments in all jurisdictions in Canada, there is still room for improvement, especially at the federal level. Most importantly, a merit-based system is needed for the promotion of judges from the trial to the appellate level; the current system represents a serious potential violation of judicial independence. Also, as the justice system continues to download more responsibilities to lower court officials, such as justices of the peace and administrative tribunals, new judicial independence issues will arise. These officials may not require the same guarantees of their independence as judges, but they do need to be in a position to be as impartial as possible in the context of the rule of law. Currently, many are not. Finally, a better understanding of judicial independence is required by some politicians, journalists, and members of interest groups, who may be tempted to pressure judges in inappropriate ways.

Procedures for appropriate judicial discipline made a quantum leap during the last three decades of the twentieth century. They still suffer from a lack of public participation, however, and the evaluation systems that are essential in any democratic institution are very rare. Effective accountability mechanisms must be developed that do not interfere with judicial independence. It is important for the courts to find ways of ensuring that witnesses, litigants, and jurors are always treated with compassion and sensitivity. Without appropriate accountability mechanisms, courts will always tend to be inward-looking, self-serving organizations rather than organizations with the highest standards of public service.

While backlogs in the processing of cases varies considerably from province to province and city to city, there are serious backlogs of both criminal and civil cases in many Canadian courts, especially in large urban centres. Although conscientious court administrators, judges, and members of the bar are attempting to find solutions, the backlogs may well continue until there is greater public participation in court administration. Mechanisms must be found to make the justice system, including the legal profession, accountable for unnecessary backlogs. But there is no magic bullet. A combination of strategies will be needed, including case management, greater judicial control over administrative issues (and appropriate judicial training in administration), and action by the law societies concerning ethical issues surrounding unnecessary delay.

CHAPTER 4

Strengths

- Merit is gradually supplanting patronage in judicial appointments at both levels.
- Canadian judges fiercely guard their independence.
- Canadian jurisprudence is at the cutting edge of judicial independence issues.
- There are procedures for dealing with complaints about the inappropriate behaviour of judges.
- Canadians trust their judges much more than their elected politicians.
- Judges are experimenting with case management to tackle unnecessary delays in the courts.

Weaknesses

- Patronage is still a factor in some judicial appointments, and in far too many appointments for justices of the peace and members of administrative tribunals.
- Canadian judges have gone to such lengths to protect their independence that they may have usurped legitimate legislative authority over their level of salary.
- No procedures are in place for judges to systematically evaluate their performance.
- Few Canadians know where to send a complaint about a judge's behaviour.
- Seriously backlogged courts still exist in large urban centres.
- Legal ethics do not clearly prohibit lawyers from using unnecessary delay as a strategy to win cases.

RESPONSIVENESS OF JUDICIAL DECISIONS TO CANADIAN DEMOCRACY 5

So far, we have focused on the analysis of the democratic character of the courts as institutions. Another important question is the extent to which judicial decisions have contributed to democracy in Canada. Although the great majority of court decisions are about which individuals or corporations win or lose in contests about the proper application of the law, some decisions have major implications for the practice of democracy itself. Through judicial review, the courts have always had an opportunity to promote – or to decline to promote – greater respect for democratic principles. The Charter of Rights, as a kind of code of ethics of democratic behaviour, has expanded the power of the courts to adjudicate issues affecting democracy.

The current debate about the relation between judicial decision making and Canadian democracy is paradoxical. Some academics on the left, such as Michael Mandel (1994), claim that judicial activism in the post-Charter era has resulted in the rich getting richer and the disadvantaged becoming more disadvantaged. At the same time, other academics on the right, such as Ted Morton and Rainer Knopff (2000; Knopff and Morton 1992), claim that Charter litigation has been "captured" primarily by left-leaning special interest groups. In a sense, both perspectives are correct, but in another sense, both miss the point.

The political ideology of liberalism, which stresses equality, freedom, and the rule of law, recognizes that the world is full of conflicting
values. It attempts to be value neutral in many respects, but not regarding the axioms that all human beings deserve to be treated as
equals and that all human beings deserve as much freedom as possible
without restricting a like freedom of their fellow human beings. These
are lofty ideals that present innumerable difficulties with regard to
their interpretation and implementation. We expect both our elected
legislators and our judges to act in the public interest to resolve conflicts as fairly as they can. Our expectations of judges are probably
higher than our expectations of politicians, however, because judges
are thought to be above political pressure, and they are presumed to
act with impartiality and wisdom. The fact that academics from the
right and the left are critical of the judiciary for failing to adopt their
particular perspectives may be an indication that the judiciary is doing a good job of steering a middle course.

A challenge that courts will always face is to avoid turning Canada
into what might be called a "juristocracy" (Hirschl 2004). Judges have
the responsibility to do their best to resolve disputes impartially and,
when they have discretion, to use that discretion in a way that con-
forms with democratic principles. When exercising discretion, however, judges always face the possibility of getting too far ahead of the
popular understanding of questions, thus discouraging the people and
their elected representatives from taking responsibility for resolving
difficult social issues. Juristocracy refers here to a judiciary that tends
to impose solutions that are not clearly required by law and are best
left to the political process to resolve.

The debate about whether the judiciary has become too interventionist centres on the most controversial decisions made by the Supreme Court and some lower courts. Most, but not all, of these decisions
involve interpretation of the Charter of Rights or the new Aboriginal
rights sections of our Constitution. This chapter focuses on about thirty
leading cases that help to illustrate the debate, by considering how responsive the Supreme Court and other courts have been to the promotion of the democratic ideals of inclusiveness and participation. First,

I will consider the cases that have implications primarily for either inclusiveness or participation, and finally the cases that straddle both concepts. My hope is that these raw materials permit readers to make up their own minds about the quality of the courts' contributions to Canadian democracy.

Very often, judicial decisions about the Charter centre on the interpretation of section 1, the "limitations clause." Section 1 states that the Charter "guarantees the rights and freedoms set out in it subject only to such reasonable limits prescribed by law as can be demonstrably justified in a free and democratic society." If the judges decide that there is a prima facie violation of a Charter right – that is, a violation on the surface without considering whether it can be justified – then they need to consider the possible implication of section 1. In the *Oakes* decision, the Supreme Court outlined how section 1 was to be applied (*R. v. Oakes* 1986). First, the judges must identify the objective of the legislation that limits a Charter right. That objective must be "substantially important" to justify limiting a right. If the first part of this test is met (as it usually is), then there is a three-pronged "proportionality test" that must also be satisfied:

- the objective identified in the first part of the test must be rationally connected to the means used to achieve it
- the means used must limit rights as little as necessary
- overall, the good achieved by the legislation in question must outweigh the harm done by limiting rights.

Decisions Relating Primarily to the Principle of Inclusiveness

SINGH ET AL. V. MINISTER OF EMPLOYMENT AND IMMIGRATION (1985)

At the time of this case, Canada's refugee determination system, although it was among the most generous in the world, did not provide for a mandatory oral hearing for refugee applicants. Satnam Singh and the other plaintiffs in this case were refugee applicants from India at a time when some elements of the Indian police and armed forces were overreacting to the Sikh insurgency by persecuting Sikhs who were not involved in the separatist movement. Canada's Refugee Status Advisory Committee did not have India on its list of refugee-producing countries, however, so when Singh and other Sikhs applied for refugee status upon their arrival in Canada, their applications were turned down and they were ordered to be deported without having had an opportunity to learn the case against them through an oral hearing process.

Madam Justice Bertha Wilson wrote the Supreme Court's decision based on the Charter of Rights. She noted that section 7 of the Charter refers to "everyone" who happens to be on Canadian soil, including refugee applicants. She concluded that Canada's refugee determination procedure at the time permitted the authorities to deport someone to a country where his or her life might be endangered, which was a clear violation of the section 7 right to "security of the person." As well, she ruled that "fundamental justice" includes the right to an oral hearing where there is an issue of credibility, and that those facing deportation have a right to know the case against them and the right to be able to respond to it. The Court did not consider any section 1 issues, as the government presented no evidence on this point.

The decision emphasizes the importance of considering fairly the plight of every individual who may be adversely affected by a governmental decision. As most refugee applicants are also members of minority groups, the decision can be seen as furthering minority rights in Canada. The decision certainly runs contrary to "majority rule," however, in that the government elected by the majority of Canadians had apparently given little thought to the possibility that its refugee-determination process might be unfair to some applicants. Given that bona fide refugee applicants are among the most vulnerable members of human society, in the democratic context they clearly deserve to be treated with concern and respect, even if elected governments think otherwise.

Andrews v. Law Society of British Columbia (1989)

Mark David Andrews was a UK citizen who had fulfilled all of the requirements for becoming a lawyer in British Columbia, except that he had not lived in Canada long enough to become a Canadian citizen. The Law Society of British Columbia, which acts on behalf of the provincial government to regulate lawyers, required all lawyers to be citizens of Canada. Its reasoning was that lawyers need to have a basic understanding of the Canadian governmental system and that citizenship is an indicator of that understanding. Andrews's view was that the citizenship requirement violated equality, as guaranteed by section 15 of the Charter, and he challenged the law society all the way to the Supreme Court.

The Court sided with Andrews. The judges concluded that while it is indeed important for lawyers to understand the machinery of Canadian government, being a citizen is no guarantee of such knowledge. Thus there is no rational connection between the objective of ensuring that lawyers understand our government, and the means used. The citizenship requirement therefore discriminates against those who desire to become lawyers based on national origin – one of the categories of discrimination prohibited by section 15. This decision can be seen as helping to promote the greater inclusion of minority groups in the legal profession.

Schachter v. Canada (1992)

In the summer of 1985, Shimon Schachter and Marcia Gilbert, a professional couple, were expecting their second child. As a lawyer, Schachter was aware that the Unemployment Insurance Act (UIA) permitted adoptive fathers and mothers to share fifteen weeks of paid parental leave between them if they had both worked long enough to qualify for benefits. In the case of birth parents, however, the fifteen weeks of parental leave was available only to mothers. Schachter saw this as a case of discrimination against birth fathers. He applied to the

Federal Court for an order to provide him with the same rights as adoptive fathers. The judge ruled that the UIA policy constituted a prima facie violation of the Charter's guarantee of equality. As in the *Andrews* case, there was no consideration of whether this violation could be justified under section 1 because the federal government presented no section 1 arguments. By way of remedy, the judge ordered that birth fathers must be treated the same as adoptive fathers if they applied for paternity benefits, though he suspended the operation of this order pending the outcome of an appeal.

This decision sent shock waves through the legal community because it was the first judicially ordered remedy that might force Parliament to spend significantly more money than it had intended. Because more fathers are employed than mothers, giving birth fathers the right to paternity leave benefits would greatly increase the cost of the parental leave program. Some considered the trial judge's decision to be an unjustified intrusion by the courts into the legislative domain. The federal government's appeal went all the way to the Supreme Court. Before the Court could hear the case, however, Parliament amended the parental leave provisions of the UIA to provide birth fathers with the same rights to share parental leave with their spouses as adoptive fathers, though the period of leave was reduced in order to keep the program within budget.

The *Schachter* case illustrates the tension between the judicial duty to enforce equality rights and Parliament's role in policy making. It also illustrates a deficiency of the litigation process involving Charter issues: our judges must rely on evidence presented by counsel rather than do their own research. Here, the judges were presented with no evidence about how differential provisions for adoptive fathers might be justified under section 1. There may have been good reasons for providing adoptive fathers only with parental leave. For example, an adoption placement usually occurs quite suddenly, compared with the nine-month wait experienced by birth parents. Adoptive parents rarely have much time to get ready for the new addition to their family unless both take time off work. The judges were forced to make a decision about an important public policy issue without all the relevant information. On the other hand, it could be argued that the *Schachter* case has resulted in the greater inclusion of birth fathers in both the benefits and burdens of child rearing.

RODRIGUEZ V. BRITISH COLUMBIA (A.G.) (1993)

In the early 1990s, Sue Rodriguez of British Columbia was suffering from amyotrophic lateral sclerosis (Lou Gehrig's disease), which attacks the motor neurons of the nervous system, eventually making it impossible for the body to function. Nearly always, the condition is fatal. Rodriguez feared that when she got to the point where she had no quality of life, the nature of the disease would leave her unable to request that she be taken off life support, or to do anything that would end her suffering. From her perspective, she wanted to die with dignity, and not put her family through the agony of watching her die a slow and painful death.

Section 241(b) of the Criminal Code makes it an offence for anyone to aid or abet a person to commit suicide. What Rodriguez wanted was a declaration from a court that in her case, section 241(b) violated her section 7 right to security of the person, and that she should therefore be exempted from it so as to be able to arrange for an assisted suicide.

In a 5-4 decision, the Supreme Court upheld the constitutionality of section 241(b). The majority held that section 241(b) did infringe Rodriguez's Charter right to security of the person because her inability to bring about an end to her life at an appropriate time would cause both unnecessary pain and psychological distress. The majority reasoned, however, that this infringement is in accord with the principles of fundamental justice because it is intended to prevent abuse. Mr. Justice John Sopinka wrote that the legislation "fulfils the government's objectives of preserving life and protecting the vulnerable ... The active participation by one person in the death of another is intrinsically, morally and legally wrong and there is no certainty that abuses can be prevented by anything less than a complete prohibition" (590, 601).

For those who are concerned about the potential for abuse of the elderly and vulnerable resulting from a law that permits assisted suicide, the *Rodriguez* decision is a victory for their inclusion in society right up to the natural ends of their lives. Conversely, for those who think that people with debilitating diseases have a right to decide when to die with dignity, the decision is a disappointment.

ELDRIDGE V. BRITISH COLUMBIA (A.G.) (1997)

The *Eldridge* case concerned whether deaf people had a right to a sign language interpreter paid for out of public funds when accessing publicly funded health services. The government of British Columbia had refused to provide Robin Eldridge with an interpreter, claiming that to provide all deaf persons with an interpreter would be too expensive. Eldridge claimed that in order to access health services that all other Canadians were provided with, an interpreter was required. Otherwise, deaf people must incur an expense that other Canadians do not. The argument was that failure to provide an interpreter amounted to discrimination based on physical disability, one of the prohibited categories of discrimination under section 15.

The Supreme Court sided with Eldridge. The Court's unanimous decision was that the failure of the provincial government to take action to provide an equal benefit to deaf people is a violation of section 15. This limitation of equality cannot be justified under section 1 because refusal to provide an interpreter does not simply minimally impair the rights of deaf people. Although the decision forces the provincial government to spend more money, these expenses may be minimal compared with the additional expenses that would have resulted from the trial court decision in *Schachter*. The *Eldridge* decision certainly promotes the inclusion of deaf people in access to the benefits of Canadian society.

SAUVÉ V. CANADA (CHIEF ELECTORAL OFFICER) (2002)

One of the most controversial recent decisions of the Supreme Court extended voting rights to all prisoners, whether in federal penitentiaries or provincial jails, no matter the reason for their incarceration. Prior to the Charter, no prisoners were allowed to vote while incarcerated in any Canadian prison, even if they were being held in custody pending a trial in which they might be found innocent, and even if they were serving a sentence of one day. In 1993 the Supreme Court ruled that this total prohibition of voting by all prisoners was "drawn too broadly" (439) and violated the Charter's section 3 right of all Canadian citizens "to vote in an election of members of the House of Commons or of a legislative assembly" (*Sauvé* v. *Canada (A.G.)* 1993). The federal government amended its approach to prohibit from voting only those prisoners sentenced to two years or more. Richard Sauvé challenged this prohibition all the way to the Supreme Court.

Preventing prisoners from voting is a prima facie violation of section 3 of the Charter, and so in order for such a prohibition to pass Charter muster, it needs to be justified as a "reasonable limit" under section 1. Lawyers for the federal government, despite having expert reports from leading political scientists, were unable to demonstrate to the Court's satisfaction that a useful public purpose was served by prohibiting prisoners from voting. First, administrative convenience seemed to be the only justification for the two-year cut-off. Second, there was no persuasive evidence that preventing prisoners serving more than two years from voting served a rehabilitative function. Third, taking away the right to vote seemed to be a punishment automatically imposed by public officials in addition to the one handed down by the court. Thus, this decision is an important one in terms of attempting to include prisoners in democratic proceedings.

Critics may well claim that the Supreme Court's decision is antidemocratic in that it goes against what the majority of Canadians probably think – that someone who offends society by breaking its laws in a serious enough way to be jailed for more than two years does not deserve to vote. (Moreover, the Court seemed to have developed stricter standards for limiting the right to vote between the 1993 and 2002 *Sauvé* cases.) But the question asked by the Supreme Court was, on what legal grounds do prisoners not deserve to vote? And counsel for the federal government could not answer to the satisfaction of the Supreme Court. In contrast, Sauvé's lawyers had expert evidence that providing prisoners with the vote was likely to help in the rehabilitative process. The great majority of prisoners will eventually be released, and it is hard to argue that being deprived of the franchise while in prison will lead to more responsible citizenship after release. The intervention of the courts in democracy through the Charter reminds us that democracy is government based on principle, not simply on emotional reactions that sometimes cannot be justified through logic or research.

OTHER DECISIONS DEALING WITH INCLUSIVENESS

Prior to the Charter, federal and provincial legislation had denied the right to vote not only to most prisoners, but also to the mentally handicapped and Canadians under eighteen. There were restrictions on registering to vote based on such matters as residency, and the permissible political activity of public servants was confined. Qualifications were placed on candidacy for public office (for example, those with significant criminal records were barred from running for certain periods), and candidates and third parties were restricted in how much they could spend during elections. Finally, discrepancies in the populations of federal and provincial constituencies meant that the more populous the constituency, the less impact a person's vote had on the electoral outcome. Since the Charter, many of these restrictions have been challenged in court or reconsidered by legislatures (Hogg 2004; Courtney 2004, ch. 2). Today, the mentally handicapped may vote if they are competent enough to register. As well, some groups are considering going to court to try to win the right to vote for those under eighteen who are informed about politics.

Litigation has resulted in the removal of many restrictions on registering to vote. Procedures have been improved to ensure that voters not present in their constituencies during an election can vote (such as students or those working outside of Canada). And although the courts have upheld rules that prohibit senior civil servants and police officers from engaging in partisan political activity, restrictions on public servants at lower levels have not withstood judicial scrutiny. Restrictions on the qualification for political office of people with records of minor breaches of legislative rules or minor criminal convictions have been removed. In general, the courts have held that the people ought to be able to decide who their representatives are.

Laws regulating involvement in election campaigns, particularly through financial contributions, have also been subject to Charter-based challenges. Since the 1960s, all political parties have been concerned about the tendency for spending during election campaigns to go through the roof, particularly with regard to television advertising. As well, the concern was that elections might be determined primarily by monied interests, resulting in subsequent public policies favouring those financing the parties. To tackle these issues, in 1974 Parliament enacted provisions to limit election spending by parties and candidates. But these spending limits were rendered ineffective by the formation of associations to advertise for or against particular candidates outside of the party umbrellas. To plug this loophole, all three major parties supported legislation in 1983 that forced nonparty groups that intended to advertise for or against particular candidates to do so under the umbrella of a party and within the overall expenditure limits. During the first two decades of the Charter, however, Canadian courts were generally receptive to the argument that restrictions on third-party spending violate the Charter (Hiebert 1996; 1990).

Just before the 1984 election, the National Citizens Coalition (NCC), a right-wing lobby group, mounted a court challenge to these provisions and won. Justice Medhurst of the Alberta Court of Queen's Bench concluded that the provisions violated the Charter's guarantee of freedom of expression, and could not be justified as a reasonable limit under section 1 because no specific examples were provided of harm done through advertising by nonparty groups (*National Citizens Coalition v. A.G. Canada* 1984). Either through neglect or design, the decision was not appealed, and as a result nonparty groups were free to spend unlimited sums during the 1984 and 1988 elections. Nonparty spending was not significant in 1984, but 1988 was a different story. Nonparty groups spent heavily to advertise for Progressive Conservative candidates because of that party's support for free trade, and this spending may well have been a deciding factor in the election.

In 2000 Parliament amended the Canada Elections Act to limit expenditures by nonparty individuals and groups to $150,000 each nationally during the thirty-day election period when party expenditures are limited (these groups could spend unlimited sums outside of this period), and to $3,000 in individual ridings. The NCC challenged the new legislation, and won in the Alberta Court of Queen's Bench in 2001 and the Alberta Court of Appeal in 2002, but this time the decision was appealed to the Supreme Court. In May 2004 the Court held in a 6-3 decision that although the legislation violated the Charter, it could be justified as a reasonable limit (*Harper* v. *Canada (A.G.)* 2004). The majority ruled that the objectives of the third-party advertising restrictions were to promote equality in electoral discourse, to protect the integrity of the party spending limits, and to promote voter confidence in the electoral process. They concluded that these objectives met all aspects of the *Oakes* test. The three dissenting judges, however, considered that although some limits on third-party spending might be justified, the amounts of $3,000 per riding and $150,000 total were "draconian." The question for readers is, has the Supreme Court decision resulted in more inclusiveness, in that Canadians who join political parties or non-party groups of modest means have a greater chance of advertising their views without being drowned out by well-financed nonparty groups? Or is there now less inclusiveness, in that legislation designed to "level the playing field" is so restrictive that citizens wanting to band together to advertise outside of party umbrellas are effectively muzzled?

The Courts and Inclusiveness

It appears that courts in recent years have often required a higher level of justification for limits to inclusiveness than legislatures have. In comparison, legislatures have dragged their feet in the promotion of inclusiveness for refugee claimants, immigrants, deaf people, and prisoners, and have been less open to more inclusive approaches to parental responsibilities. As well, they have been slower to respond to legitimate complaints about restrictions on voting and candidacy. On the other hand, Parliament's efforts to reform electoral financing to reduce the influence of money on electoral outcomes was at first hobbled by court decisions. In the end, the legislation that limits third-party spending probably benefited from judicial intervention, but it is unfortunate that it took two decades for the dialogue between the courts and Parliament to resolve the issue.

Participation

Canadian courts have made significant contributions to the democratic principle of participation, both before and since the entrenchment of the Charter.

THE DUFF DOCTRINE

In 1937 the Social Credit legislature in Alberta enacted a package of legislation intended to put Social Credit theory into effect. One of the enactments, the Accurate News and Information Act, informally known as the "Alberta Press Bill," gave a government agency the power to censor newspapers that criticized Social Credit policies and theories about banks and the economy. The package of legislation was referred by the federal government to the Supreme Court for an opinion on its constitutionality.

The Court found the Alberta Press Bill unconstitutional because it was part of a series of laws designed to regulate banking, a federal responsibility (*Reference re Alberta Statutes* 1938). Chief Justice Sir Lyman Duff, however, considered the Alberta Press Bill so repugnant to democratic principles that he provided additional reasons. He wrote that because of the preamble to the 1867 Constitution, which states that the new country has "a Constitution similar in Principle to that of the United Kingdom," the civil liberties that existed in the United Kingdom in 1867 had been imported into the Canadian Constitution. Duff held that our Constitution thus protects freedom of the press and speech. As well, he noted that the House of Commons is a "representative" body, and the

Constitution therefore "contemplates a parliament working under the influence of public opinion and public discussion ... It is axiomatic that the practice of this right of free public discussion of public affairs, notwithstanding its incidental mischiefs, is the breath of life for parliamentary institutions" (133). This reasoning became known as the Duff doctrine, and it was eventually endorsed by a majority of judges on the Supreme Court during the Charter era (*OPSEU* v. *Ontario (A.G.)* 1987; *Reference re Remuneration of Judges* 1997). The Duff doctrine is one of the cornerstones of public participation in the Canadian polity.

PREVENTION OF ABUSE OF POWER

An abuse of power occurs when a government official acts without legal sanction and causes harm or suffering as a result. Abuses of power can often result in arbitrary restrictions on political participation.

The best-known examples of judicial action to prevent abuse of power occurred during the government of authoritarian Quebec premier Maurice Duplessis. The Duplessis government was intolerant of groups that were unpopular or not part of the mainstream. In the early 1950s, the Duplessis government enacted the "padlock law," which authorized police to lock up the premises of individuals or groups that were distributing what they considered to be subversive literature. In 1957 the Supreme Court struck down the padlock law because it interfered with the federal government's criminal law power (*Switzman* v. *Elbling and Quebec (A.G.)* 1957). This case is an example of the use of judicial discretion because the Court could have as easily decided that the padlock law was a valid exercise of the province's power over property and civil rights (s. 92 (13), Constitution Act, 1867).

An even more prominent example of judicial intervention to challenge to abuse of power is the case of *Roncarelli* v. *Duplessis* (1959). The Duplessis government had taken a number of steps to try to stop the Jehovah's Witnesses from proselytising in Quebec. Roncarelli, a relatively well-to-do human rights advocate who owned a restaurant in Montreal, would post bail for Jehovah's Witnesses who had been arrested. Duplessis personally and arbitrarily revoked Roncarelli's liquor licence so that his restaurant would be less attractive to customers. A prominent civil libertarian, Frank Scott, helped Roncarelli challenge Duplessis's action in court. Roncarelli scored a victory when the Supreme Court declared that no legislation gave the premier the power to revoke Roncarelli's liquor licence. Even the premier is subject to the rule of law.

R. V. MORGENTALER (1988)

The issue in the *Morgentaler* case was whether section 251 of the Criminal Code - which prohibited abortions unless they were carried out by a qualified doctor in an approved hospital with approval from the hospital's abortion committee - violated the Charter's guarantee of security of the person in section 7. The Supreme Court ruled 5-2 that section 251 violated the Charter, but the judges in the majority gave three different sets of reasons. Chief Justice Brian Dickson argued that procedures set up by section 251 were so cumbersome and restrictive that they caused unnecessary psychological stress to pregnant women applying for an abortion, and that they were not rationally connected to the goal of section 251, which he said was to protect the life and health of pregnant women. Justice Beetz wrote that the complex administrative procedures required by section 251 served to protect neither the fetus nor the pregnant woman's life or health. Justice Wilson ruled that the mechanisms set up by section 251 constituted an unacceptable affront to the dignity of women and freedom of conscience, but that the state had a right to regulate abortions beginning some time in the second trimester. The two dissenting judges considered that the abortion issue was so political that the courts ought to leave its regulation entirely up to Parliament.

In essence, the majority decisions in *Morgentaler* left plenty of scope for Parliament to regulate abortion, so long as the procedures it established were demonstrably and rationally connected to clearly defined and legitimate objectives, and women's rights were limited as little as necessary to achieve those objectives. By leaving such a wide scope for Parliament to act, the Court was deferring to the political process, and encouraging public participation in the resolution of this controversial issue. At the same time, the Court emphasized that women must be treated with respect, and that only legislation that eliminated unnecessary distress would pass muster. In 1989, the House of Commons passed new abortion legislation that probably would have survived a Charter challenge but was rejected in the Senate by one vote. This absence of federal legislation has meant that the regulation of abortion now depends on provincial health legislation, which sometimes entails greater restrictions than those under section 251 (Gavigan 1992). No federal government has had the stomach to tackle the abortion issue since, and so the Supreme Court's attempt to hand it back to the political process, as long as minimum standards of fundamental justice are met, has so far failed. Should the Supreme Court's intervention be seen as promoting democratic participation, or inadvertently restricting it?

RJR-MacDonald Inc. v. Canada (A.G.) (1995)

In this decision, the Supreme Court of Canada struck down the 1988 Tobacco Products Control Act because it violated freedom of expression and did not meet the section 1 tests for rationality or for limiting rights as little as necessary. The 1988 legislation required unattributed health warnings on all tobacco product packages, prohibited all advertising of tobacco products, and limited the promotion of events by tobacco companies. The majority found that these restrictions were overbroad, and that the government could achieve its objectives without such sweeping prohibitions. The Court hinted, however, that it would uphold similar legislation if it were limited to prohibiting "lifestyle advertising," or advertising directed at children. In 1997 Parliament enacted a new Tobacco Act that attempted to comply with the Court's guidelines. The new legislation prohibited tobacco advertising directed toward young people but allowed non-lifestyle tobacco advertising directed toward adults. As well, it gradually phased out sponsorships of events by tobacco companies. At the time of writing, this new legislation has not been successfully challenged in court.

From one perspective, it could be argued that the 1988 legislation that limited tobacco advertising went further than necessary to achieve the government's objective of discouraging smoking, and that the current legislation meets the government's objectives while respecting freedom of expression. Janet Hiebert (2002), however, argues that by simply complying with the guidelines established by the Supreme Court in the *RJR-MacDonald* decision, Parliament took the path of least resistance. Instead, a parliamentary committee could have examined the empirical evidence about the relation between advertising and smoking, and drafted new legislation based on the evidence, which might not have complied with the Supreme Court's edicts. If the new legislation were challenged, government lawyers could rely on the committee's report to justify the legislation under section 1. Democratic participation implies that elected members have a duty to enact legislation in the public interest based on careful research, rather than bowing to judicial interpretation. Indeed, the *Mills* case is an example of Parliament successfully following such a strategy.

R. V. MILLS (1999)

The issue in the *Mills* case was the balance between the right to a fair trial of persons accused of sexual assault, and the right to privacy of victims of sexual assault in relation to their medical records and records kept by therapists. In *R. v. O'Connor* (1995), a five-judge majority in the Supreme Court struck down the existing legislation for erring too much on the side of privacy, and it established a test for evaluating future legislation of this nature. In essence, the Court concluded that accused persons or their counsel must demonstrate to the trial judge that the private record of the alleged victim (to which the accused would have access) is necessary for the defence and that its production would not unreasonably affect the alleged victim's dignity or security of the person.

In 1997, after an extensive investigation by government officials and a legislative committee, Parliament enacted new legislation (Hiebert 2002). If an accused person wanted to use an alleged victim's private records as evidence, a judge would need to hold a closed hearing in which the judge would review the private record to determine its relevancy, without revealing the private record to the accused's lawyer.

This procedure was more restrictive to the rights of the accused than contemplated by the Supreme Court's majority in *O'Connor,* but was very similar to the position adopted by the *O'Connor* minority.

When the new legislation was tested in the *Mills* case, the Supreme Court majority upheld it although it did not comply entirely with the test in the *O'Connor* decision. The Court referred to Peter Hogg's "dialogue" thesis (Hogg and Thornton 1999). According to this thesis, in most cases where the courts have struck down legislation, the appropriate legislature has re-enacted revised legislation that overcomes the human rights shortcomings identified by the Court, while achieving its policy goals. Hogg and Thornton examined sixty-five federal and provincial laws that had been struck down partly or entirely by the courts. They showed that 80 percent had been revised and re-enacted. In 75 percent, the legislative response came within two years. In *Mills,* the Court showed that through such "dialogue" it could learn from the legislature as well as the other way around.

F.L. Morton (2002, 603-8) has claimed that the intervention of courts in public policy is more of a monologue than a dialogue because the courts always have the last word as to the constitutionality of legislation. He claims this tends to inhibit public participation, through electoral politics, in the policy-making process. But if the courts show a willingness to defer to the legislature whenever the legislature can work out a thoughtful balance of rights that is based on a research process not open to the courts, is the legislative branch really inhibited?

Charter Cases Dealing with Both Inclusiveness and Participation

R. v. Big M Drug Mart Ltd. (1985) and R. v. Edwards Books and Art Ltd. (1986)

As a result of the religious wars between Roman Catholics and Protestants that followed the Reformation, it became accepted by the eighteenth century that religious beliefs could not be compelled, nor should this be attempted. But it often takes time for the legislative framework to catch up to higher social standards of rights and freedoms.

Until 1985, the Lord's Day Act was valid federal legislation copied from a British statute of 1677 – a year when freedom of religion had not yet been fully recognized. The Lord's Day Act prohibited, under threat of criminal sanction, the operation of certain kinds of businesses on Sundays, the sabbath for most Christians. The Lord's Day Act had been challenged under the Canadian Bill of Rights, but the challenge was rejected by the Supreme Court primarily because of its unwillingness to strike down legislation pursuant to the bill, which was an ordinary statute without constitutional status (*Robertson and Rosetanni* v. *The Queen* 1963).

After the Charter came into effect, the Lord's Day Act was challenged once again by Big M Drug Mart of Calgary. When the case got to the Supreme Court, Chief Justice Dickson (who had been chancellor of the Anglican Diocese of Rupert's Land) wrote the main opinion that struck down the act as a violation of freedom of religion. He noted that one of the purposes of freedom of religion is to protect "religious minorities from the threat of the 'tyranny of the majority'" (337). Therefore, to compel all Canadians to comply with the practices of one religion was not only a violation of freedom of religion, but it also represented a misguided understanding of Christian teachings. Enlightened Christians had come to understand that "attempts to compel belief or practice denied the reality of individual conscience and dishonoured the God that had planted it in His creatures" (345). The decision striking down the Lord's Day Act certainly paved the way for hundreds of thousands of Canadians who are not Christian to feel included in Canadian society, and may also have had the effect of encouraging more participation in political institutions by religious minorities.

The Big M decision left open the question of whether legislation creating a weekly day of rest could pass Charter muster without inadvertently violating the principle of freedom of religion. That question was answered by the Supreme Court in 1986 in the *Edwards Books and Art* decision. Like the Lord's Day Act, Ontario's Retail Business Holidays Act required most retail businesses to be closed on Sundays. The act, however, was secular: its purpose was to ensure a weekly common pause day to provide an opportunity for families to spend time together. Exceptions built into the legislation allowed entertainment facilities and corner stores to remain open. As well, in deference to businesspeople whose holy day is Saturday, small businesses were allowed to operate on Sundays and close on Saturdays instead.

The owners of Edwards Books and Art argued that the act represented an indirect violation of freedom of religion, in that it had the same impact as the Lord's Day Act. The Supreme Court agreed that the act did represent an indirect interference with freedom of religion, because the common pause day placed a greater burden on those whose religion specified a holy day other than Sunday. The majority ruled, however, that this violation could be justified under section 1. The purpose of the act – to provide a common pause day – was "pressing and substantial." This objective is rationally connected to the means used, the Court ruled, because retail workers were often not unionized and therefore had difficulty negotiating a common pause day with employers, and this justified government intervention. As well, the exceptions to the Sunday-closing rule allowed for quality leisure activities for families.

This decision clearly promoted inclusiveness in Canadian society. The Court reminded elected officials that their laws must take into account the religious convictions of Canadians of all faiths. At the same time, by upholding the Ontario Retail Business Holidays Act, the Court left provincial legislatures with a wide scope for developing a policy for a common pause day that accommodates a variety of religious practices. This ruling might also have encouraged greater public participation in the development of provincial policies regarding common pause day policy.

R. v. KEEGSTRA (1990) AND R. v. ZUNDEL (1992)

The Supreme Court's decisions in the *Keegstra* and *Zundel* cases are the leading examples of the Court's approach to hate speech. Both Jim Keegstra and Ernst Zundel had disseminated anti-Semitic materials and both claimed that the Holocaust, as the great majority of historians understand it, is an exaggeration. Keegstra was a high school teacher in a small Alberta town. He taught his anti-Semitic views to his students and expected them to absorb his lessons as historical facts. Ernst Zundel published his views in various tracts that he produced, and through the Internet. The cases are different in that Keegstra was charged with violating section 319(2) of the Criminal Code – "wilfully promoting hatred against an identifiable group" – while Zundel was charged with "spreading false news" contrary to section 181 of the Criminal Code. Keegstra and Zundel were charged under different sections of the Criminal Code not because of any coordinated strategy on the part of the police, but because the police and prosecutors in Alberta and Ontario had different perspectives on how best to get a conviction.

Keegstra was convicted at trial in the mid-1980s, but his appeal took him all the way to the Supreme Court, which upheld his conviction in a 4-3 decision. The majority declared that although section 319(2) violates freedom of expression, this violation can be justified under section 1. They reasoned that the objective of section 319(2) – to prevent harm caused by hate propaganda – is an important government objective rationally connected to the outlawing of hate speech. The judges referred to the anti-Semitic hate speech that was rampant in Germany before and during the Second World War, and which led to the Holocaust, as proof of the rational connection. The dissenting judges, meanwhile, saw no evidence of actual or threatened violence that had resulted from Keegstra's teachings. They noted that the social conditions in Canada in the 1980s were quite different from those in Germany during the 1930s and 1940s. As well, they argued that the best way to put an end to hate speech is to allow it to occur in the open, where fair-minded people can persuasively contradict it. To suppress it might drive it underground, thus increasing the chances of violence.

Zundel, on the other hand, won his case in the Supreme Court. Section 181 of the Criminal Code states that "every one who wilfully publishes a statement, tale or news that he knows is false and causes or is likely to cause injury or mischief to a public interest is guilty of an indictable offence and liable to imprisonment." Once again the Supreme Court was divided 4-3. Justice L'Heureux-Dubé had voted with the majority in *Keegstra* to uphold section 319(2), but she switched sides in *Zundel* to vote for striking down section 181. Except for the addition of L'Heureux-Dubé, the majority in *Zundel* is made up of the same judges as the minority in *Keegstra*. They wrote that the purpose of freedom of expression is not only to promote the search for the truth but also to promote public participation in politics and society, and to promote self-fulfilment. They wrote that expression often includes ideas that the majority may find offensive or wrong, and that freedom of expression does not depend on the content of the expression. The majority traced section 181 back to medieval legislation intended to uphold the dignity of the English nobility. They ruled that this is no longer an important government objective, and therefore the legislation fails the reasonable limits test under section 1. Even if the legislation were considered to have the modern objective of promoting social harmony, however, the majority ruled that this objective is not rationally connected to giving the police the power to prosecute people for "spreading false news." This power might be abused, and could have a chilling effect, resulting in social unrest.

Did the *Keegstra* and *Zundel* decisions promote inclusiveness and participation? Some might argue that the *Keegstra* decision promoted inclusiveness by making it possible for the state to intervene to stop the most egregious examples of hate speech, and thus protect the most vulnerable groups in society. Others might hold that by allowing the state to suppress free speech in some cases, the Court promoted a kind of political correctness that might eventually backfire against the very groups that the hate speech law is intended to help (Newman 2004). The extremely close decisions in both *Keegstra* and *Zundel* illustrate the complexity of the issue and summarize the divided viewpoints about how best to protect the vulnerable and promote inclusion. Nevertheless, the publicity surrounding both cases stimulated an enormous amount of public debate about the hate speech issue. This unintended consequence of the judicial process is healthy for participatory democracy. And although the *Keegstra* decision leaves open the possibility that the state might intervene to suppress hate speech, prosecutions under the hate speech provision of the Criminal Code cannot proceed without the permission of the provincial attorney general. As the new century progresses, that permission is almost never forth-coming, perhaps a reflection of the outcome of the public debate that ensued from the *Keegstra* and *Zundel* decisions.

REFERENCE RE PROV. ELECTORAL BOUNDARIES (SASK.) (1991)

In 1989 the Saskatchewan legislature proclaimed new rules for setting electoral boundaries. (Both before and after this change, Saskatchewan had one of the fairest systems of electoral districts, that is, closest to "one person, one vote.") Henceforth, boundaries in urban areas would have to correspond with municipal ones. As well, a fixed number of rural seats was established in the southern part of the province in spite of the increasing urban population. The result was that the variance between the most and least populous constituencies, and between them and the provincial average, grew to as much as 25 percent, compared with only about 15 percent under the old system. Some city dwellers claimed that this increased underrepresentation of urban voters vio-lated the right to vote guaranteed by section 3 of the Charter, as well as its equality guarantees. A reference question from the Saskatchewan government made its way to the Supreme Court of Canada.

The decision of the majority of six judges deferred to the Saskatch-ewan legislature's new plan. Justice McLachlin wrote that deviations from equal representation might be justified by factors such as geog-raphy, the need to include minorities, history, diversity, and commu-nity interests. In this case, geography, community interests, and population growth patterns justified constituency boundaries that re-sulted in rural voters being significantly overrepresented in the south-ern part of the province. The sparsely populated north had been allocated two seats, which meant that northern voters were even more overrepresented than rural southerners. Because of a small population distributed over a vast region, however, there was no other practical alternative to promote effective representation.

The three dissenters, led by Justice Peter Cory, had no difficulty jus-tifying the overrepresentation in the two northern ridings. But in the south, they could find no compelling reasons for increasing the underrepresentation of urban voters. They wrote that arbitrary limits to voting parity constituted an abrogation of the right to vote.

By giving wide scope to the legislature's decision to increase the overrepresentation of rural voters, the Supreme Court has clearly promoted inclusiveness for rural voters and has encouraged their participation in policy making. But has the Supreme Court also unfairly diminished inclusiveness for urban voters, and discouraged their participation because of their increased underrepresentation?

R. v. BUTLER (1992) AND R. v. SHARPE (2001)

Donald Victor Butler of Winnipeg was convicted under section 163 of the Criminal Code for selling and renting hard-core pornographic videos and magazines. Section 163 prohibits the sale of obscene materials where a dominant characteristic of the material is the undue exploitation of sex, or sex combined with crime, horror, cruelty, or violence. Butler argued that section 163 violates the guarantee of freedom of expression in the Charter.

The trial judge ruled that the application of section 163 is restricted because of the Charter, and so although Butler had been charged with over one hundred offences, he was convicted on only eight counts. When the case reached the Supreme Court, in a unanimous decision the Court clarified the meaning of obscenity, and then ordered Butler to be tried again according to this revised definition. The Court held that section 163 infringed the Charter, but that a carefully tailored definition of obscenity constitutes a reasonable limit under section 1.

Justice Sopinka wrote that material is obscene if its exploitation of sex is "undue" according to a "community standards test." This test is not what Canadians would tolerate for themselves, but what they would tolerate others being exposed to, considering the harm to society that might result. It is important that those involved in producing the potentially obscene material consent to its production, but consent is not necessarily determinative of whether the community standards test is passed. As well, if the materials in question are claimed to be works of art, then they must pass an "internal necessities" test: is the material really required for a serious treatment of a theme, or is it just an excuse for the undue exploitation of sex? If in doubt about this, judges should err on side of freedom of expression. Sopinka wrote that materials that combine sex and violence would nearly always constitute obscenity. Sex that is dehumanizing would be considered obscene if the risk of harm to society is considered substantial. Finally, sex that is not violent or degrading is usually tolerated unless it involves children.

The Court ruled that the prohibition of obscene materials is a reasonable limit to freedom of expression because the objective, the prevention of harm, is pressing and substantial. There is a rational connection between the suppression of obscene materials and preventing harm. Freedom of expression is minimally impaired, because section 163 can be used to prohibit only truly harmful material, and the internal necessities test allows for artistic expression. Finally, the public good accomplished by section 163 outweighs the harm caused by censoring freedom of expression.

The *Butler* decision did not deal with what stricter limits could apply to pornographic materials involving children, which brings us to the *Sharpe* case. In the late 1990s, John Robin Sharpe of Vancouver was charged with possession of pornographic materials under a subsection of section 163 that prohibited the possession and distribution of child pornography. Sharpe was an admitted pedophile, and many of the materials in his possession and that he had distributed to others were stories and drawings that he himself had produced. Sharpe argued that section 163 was overbroad and interfered unnecessarily with his freedom of expression. Sharpe won at his trial and in the BC Court of Appeal – leaving many members of the public aghast – and the Crown appealed to the Supreme Court. The Court held that the anti-child pornography legislation was valid, but the majority "read in" two restrictions. First, it declared that the legislation could not be applied to self-created expressive material: i.e., "any written material or visual representation created by the accused alone, and held by the accused alone, exclusively for his/her own personal use." Second, the Court stated that the legislation does not cover private recordings of lawful sexual activity "created by or depicting the accused, provided it does not depict unlawful sexual activity and is held by the accused exclusively for private use" (49). (The judges had been presented with a hypothetical scenario in which two seventeen-year-olds, lawfully married but still legally "children," might videotape themselves having sex and thus run afoul of section 163.) In its decision, the Court attempted to defer to Parliament's desire to prevent the distribution of child pornography, while at the same time restrict the application of section 163 so that it would not be used to invade privacy unnecessarily.

Most Canadians probably approve of the anti-obscenity provisions of the Criminal Code, and clearly the great majority support the anti-child-pornography sections. By upholding these provisions, the Supreme Court deferred to the will of the majority. By attempting to limit the application of section 163 only to invasions of privacy that are necessary to prevent social harm, however, the Court also tried to ensure that even some of the less savoury people in society are included in the ambit of the Charter's protections.

Symes v. Canada (1993) and Thibaudeau v. Canada (1995)

In the early 1980s, the Income Tax Act allowed the deduction of child care expenses from income, but only to a maximum of between about $1,000 and $4,000. Child care expenses might include the cost of day care or a nanny, and these expenses are normally much higher than the maximum allowed by the act. Elizabeth Symes, a Toronto lawyer, spent between $10,000 and $13,500 each year between 1982 and 1985 on a nanny to take care of her children so that she could continue her career. Symes felt that not being able to deduct all of her child care expenses from her income constituted discrimination based on sex. This is because in most situations, if the family cannot afford the full cost of day care or a nanny, usually the mother ends up working part-time or not at all, while the father continues his career. If the full cost of care could be deducted from income, then mothers would have an equal ability to have children and also continue their careers. Symes appealed her income tax assessment to the Trial Division of the Federal Court and won; the federal government appealed all the way to the Supreme Court.

Mr. Justice Frank Iacobucci wrote the opinion for the seven judges who supported the validity of the legislation. He argued that Symes had presented no convincing empirical evidence that a higher child care deduction would lead more women to choose to pursue their careers. As well, he concluded that there was no hard evidence that women are more disadvantaged than men by the limit to the child care deduction. The two women on the Court, Justices McLachlin and L'Heureux-Dubé, dissented, concluding that because of the legislation, the cost of child care is disproportionately borne by women – a violation of the Charter's equality guarantee.

The Income Tax Act was also the object of challenge by Suzanne Thibaudeau. When she divorced in 1987, she had been awarded custody of her two children, aged six and eight. Her former husband was ordered to pay alimony of about $14,000 a year for the maintenance of the children. At the time, the Income Tax Act stipulated that the spouse (usually the mother) receiving maintenance payments must claim these payments as income, while the spouse making the payments could deduct the payments from his or her income. Because Thibaudeau earned more than her former husband and was in a higher tax bracket than average, she had to pay tax on the alimony received at a higher rate than the average tax on most alimony payments. Even though the court took this anomalous situation into account when calculating the alimony, Thibaudeau thought that the system was unfair. She and her ex-husband were paying a higher proportion of their combined incomes in tax than the majority of divorced couples. Thus, they had proportionately less money left over for child care than divorced couples in which the man had the higher income. In protest, she filed an income tax return in 1989 that did not include the alimony. Revenue Canada reassessed the return, and she eventually ended up in the Supreme Court.

Thibaudeau's main argument was that forcing the spouse receiving the alimony always to pay the tax on it, rather than the spouse with the lower income, constitutes discrimination based on sex. Her view was that the provisions of the Income Tax Act regarding maintenance payments were based on a sexual stereotype – that women, who usually get custody of children after a divorce, usually earn less than men.

The majority of five male judges did not see a violation of equality here. They reasoned that all divorced families are treated the same: the spouse making the maintenance payment gets the deduction. Overall, because fathers generally earn more than mothers, this results in less tax being paid than if the spouse paying out the alimony always had to pay the tax on it. Judges would take into account anomalous situations in determining the amount of alimony.

The dissenters, as in *Symes*, were the two women judges: McLachlin and L'Heureux-Dubé. They saw the Income Tax Act as creating an unintentional violation of equality because of the assumptions that most custodial spouses would be women, and that their income would generally be lower than that of men. As well, women like Thibaudeau would have to hire a lawyer and put up with the delays and cost of the legal system in order to win fair treatment as their incomes rose. McLachlin and L'Heureux-Dubé argued that the violation of equality could not be justified under section 1. In the case of women like Thibaudeau, there is clearly no rational connection between the objective of the impugned provision – to place more child support money in the hands of the separated or divorced parents – and the means used. As well, Thibaudeau's rights are not minimally restricted, as there are other ways of treating divorced couples equitably that are more fair.

Ironically, it appeared that federal officials anticipated losing the case. Shortly after the *Thibaudeau* decision, the government announced that it planned to amend the Income Tax Act so that there would be no tax deduction for maintenance payments, and no taxation of these payments. This took effect in 1997. The government promised that the resulting increased tax revenues would be earmarked for programs to support children.

From the perspective of those who believe that parts of the Income Tax Act are based on sexual stereotypes, the majority decisions in *Symes* and *Thibaudeau* have failed to promote inclusiveness, although the *Thibaudeau* case likely triggered the federal government's 1997 amendments to the legislation. On the other hand, the Court's deference to Parliament in these cases could be considered an endorsement of popular participation in policy making, in that elected officials ought to get the last word regarding complex taxation policies.

REFERENCE RE SECESSION OF QUEBEC (1998)

This decision may well represent the Court's most important contribution to the Canadian approach to the democratic process. The events leading up to the this case date from the defeat of the Charlottetown Accord in a national referendum in 1992. The Charlottetown Accord, as well as the failed Meech Lake Accord before it, would have enabled Quebec to ratify the constitutional changes that resulted in the Charter of Rights and the constitutional amending formulas of 1982 – changes that every provincial government except Quebec's had approved. The failure of the Charlottetown process provided an ideal opportunity for the Parti Québécois government of Jacques Parizeau to call a provincial referendum on Quebec secession in 1995. The original strategy of the federal government of Prime Minister Jean Chrétien to stay out of the debate in Quebec backfired; the "yes" side came within six-tenths of a percent of winning on 30 October 1995. Subsequently, the Chrétien government became much tougher toward Quebec regarding the secession issue, although a more cooperative approach was adopted regarding intergovernmental relations.

This new strategy led the federal government to send a reference question to the Supreme Court of Canada in 1997 asking, first, whether the Constitution gives the Quebec government the right to implement the unilateral secession of Quebec, and second, whether international law provides that right. The decision, rendered in 1998, was "of the Court," a procedure sometimes used by the judges to demonstrate their single-mindedness.

The Court answered the first question in the negative, underlining the legal necessity for a province to use the constitutional amending provisions (which involve obtaining the agreement of the other provinces and the federal government) if it wishes to secede. But the Court didn't stop there, as it might have; it went on to state that the four foundational principles underlying Canada's Constitution are federalism, the rule of law, minority rights, and democracy, and noted that the arguments in support of unilateral secession were primarily based on the principle of democracy. Democracy, the judges wrote, "means more than simple majority rule ... Constitutional jurisprudence [shows that] democracy exists in the larger context of other constitutional values" (para. 149), such as "respect for the inherent dignity of the human person" (para. 64). The Court added that "a functioning democracy requires a continuous process of discussion ... compromise, negotiation, and deliberation. Inevitably, there will be dissenting voices. A democratic system of government is committed to considering those dissenting voices" (para. 68). Therefore, based on basic democratic principles, the Court concluded that "a clear majority vote in Québec on a clear question in favour of secession" would oblige the federal government and the other provinces to negotiate Quebec's secession in good faith (para. 150). The terms "a clear question" and "a clear majority" were intentionally not defined; these needed to be determined, if the need arose, by the political process (para. 151).

In answering the second question, the Court wrote that a right to secession arises under international law only where "a people" is governed as part of a colonial empire, "is subject to alien subjugation, domination or exploitation" (para. 133), and possibly is denied the "meaningful exercise of its right to self-determination" within the federation (para. 134). These factors certainly did not apply in Quebec. Canada is "entitled to maintain its territorial integrity under international law and to have that territorial integrity recognized by other States. Québec does not meet the threshold of a colonial people or an oppressed people" (para. 154).

The Supreme Court's intervention on the Quebec secession issue outlines a way in which Quebec or any other province could attempt to secede from Canada in a constitutional way. Moreover, the decision engages in the consideration of the democratic norms of participation (discussion, negotiation, compromise, and elections) and inclusiveness (the protection of minority rights, and the promotion of the inherent dignity of all citizens of Canada and Quebec). This decision is extremely innovative, and some might argue that this decision alone might justify the Court's unofficial role as Canada's democratic conscience.

VRIEND V. ALBERTA (1998), M. V. H. (1999), AND HALPERN ET AL. (2003)

The *Vriend* case was the first of three important cases in Canada that resulted in major advances for the inclusion of homosexuals in Canada's antidiscrimination regime. The case concerned a lab coordinator employed by a religious community college in Edmonton that did not approve of homosexuality. Delwin Vriend worked his way up to a full-time, permanent position in 1988. In 1990 the president of the college learned that Vriend was a homosexual. Vriend confirmed this and was fired. He appealed to the Alberta Human Rights Commission, but was told that the commission could not consider his case because Alberta's human rights act did not prohibit discrimination based on sexual orientation. Vriend and others then went to court to request a declaration that the omission of sexual orientation is a violation of the Charter's guarantee of equality. The trial judge agreed with Vriend, and "read in" sexual orientation as one of the prohibited grounds of discrimination. The Crown appealed, and the case eventually ended up in the Supreme Court. The nine judges were unanimous in supporting Vriend's position.

The main decision, written by Chief Justice Antonio Lamer, held that the failure to include sexual orientation in a provincial human rights act denies the equal protection of the law. Turning to the section 1 analysis, the Crown did not present a convincing argument that there is a pressing and substantial objective in excluding homosexuals. Lamer wrote that human rights legislation is designed to protect people from being discriminated against because of irrelevant personal characteristics. Thus, it is not rational to exclude homosexuals from such legislation. Clearly, the rights of homosexuals are not minimally impaired by the exclusion, and the Crown failed to demonstrate that any good is achieved by excluding homosexuals. Lamer stated that the proper remedy is to interpret the act as if sexual orientation is included as a prohibited grounds of discrimination.

This decision was extremely controversial in Alberta. For a few days, Premier Ralph Klein's cabinet contemplated whether to re-enact the legislation with a section 33 override. (Section 33 of the Charter permits provincial legislatures and Parliament to enact legislation that might violate the parts of the Charter dealing with fundamental freedoms, legal rights, and equality rights for five-year periods, as long as a clause is inserted into the legislation stating that the legislation is valid "notwithstanding" these sections of the Charter.) In the end, after public opinion polls in Alberta indicated a fair amount of support for the Supreme Court decision, the cabinet decided not to interfere. Premier Klein announced that although the inclusion of homosexuals in the legislation was not a decision that the government would voluntarily have made, it had decided to defer to the Court.

The second case, *M.* v. *H.,* concerned two Ontario lesbians who lived together from 1982 to 1992. They ran an advertising business together, which was at first quite successful but then began to lose money during the economic downturn. H. had put more money into the business than M. When their relationship fell apart, M. made a claim for part of H.'s assets under Ontario's Family Law Act, which requires more or less an equal division of assets if a marriage breaks up. The Family Law Act allowed a former spouse to claim support from the other former spouse and defined a spouse as someone who is legally married or a man and a woman who are not married but who have cohabited continuously for a period of at least three years in a conjugal relationship. M. applied for a motion that the definition of spouse offended the guarantee of equality in the Charter and that therefore homosexual couples should be included in the definition.

The motions judge agreed with this argument, essentially for the same reasons supplied by the Supreme Court in *Vriend.* H. appealed to the Ontario Court of Appeal, and lost. At that point, M. and H. decided to stop fighting and live with the decision, but the attorney general of Ontario appealed to the Supreme Court and lost in 1999. As in *Vriend,* Chief Justice Lamer wrote the majority opinion, and his reasoning was similar to that in the earlier case. Gay and lesbian couples, he wrote, are disadvantaged and discriminated against by not being included in the Family Law Act. In the section 1 analysis, Lamer could find no rational connection between the Family Law Act's objectives – to provide equitable resolution of economic disputes when conjugal relationships break down – and the exclusion of gays and lesbians from the act. He noted that the rights of gays and lesbians were not minimally impaired by their exclusion, and the harm done by their exclusion was clear. The Court declared invalid the act's definition of spouse and gave the Ontario legislature six months to amend the legislation.

In June 2003, the Ontario Court of Appeal in the *Halpern* case declared that gay and lesbian couples have the right to marry. The case was initiated by Hedy Halpern and her partner, Colleen Rogers, along with seven other lesbian or gay couples, who had requested a declaration that Ontario's common law definition of marriage – a union between "one man and one woman" – constituted a violation of the Charter's equality guarantee. The Court of Appeal panel, which included Chief Justice Roy McMurtry (former Conservative attorney general of Ontario), and Mr. Justice James MacPherson (former dean of Osgoode Hall Law School), followed the reasoning in *Vriend* and *M. v. H.* They redefined marriage as "the voluntary union for life of two persons to the exclusion of all others."

Turning to the section 1 test, the judges concluded that the Crown had provided no persuasive reasons as to why the traditional definition of marriage was pressing and substantial. If the objective of the traditional definition of marriage is procreation and child rearing, the appeal court panel could find no rational connection with the exclusion of homosexuals from marriage, because homosexual couples can adopt children or have children through surrogacy and donor insemination. If the objective is the promotion of companionship, there was no evidence that homosexual couples could not form long-lasting and loving relationships. The complete exclusion of homosexuals from marriage clearly does not minimally impair their rights, and the Court could find no evidence of a benefit to society in the exclusion. The judges reasoned that the inclusion of same-sex couples in the institution of marriage in no way interferes with the nature of marriage for heterosexual couples or with the religious institution of marriage. The court ordered the immediate implementation of the new common law definition of marriage in Ontario. Similar decisions were made by the BC Court of Appeal in May 2003 (*EGALE Canada Inc.* v. *Canada (A.G.)* 2003), and by the Quebec Superior Court in 2002 (*Hendricks* v. *Quebec (A.G.)* 2002), although the implementation of the Quebec decision was suspended until September 2004.

In response to these court decisions, in the fall of 2003 the federal cabinet drafted legislation that defined marriage for civil purposes as "the lawful union of two persons to the exclusion of all others," and also declared, "Nothing in this Act affects the freedom of officials of religious groups to refuse to perform marriages that are not in accordance with their religious beliefs." The cabinet sent a reference question to the Supreme Court to request an opinion on the constitutionality of the new legislation. The Court released its decision in December 2004, confirming that the legislation is within the competence of the federal Parliament, that it does not violate the Charter of Rights and Freedoms, and that thanks to the guarantee of freedom of religion in the Charter, no religious official can be compelled to perform a same-sex marriage that is against his or her religious beliefs (*Reference re Same-Sex Marriage,* 2004). In February 2005, the government introduced legislation to permit same-sex marriage. After some stormy debate, the legislation passed through Parliament and received royal assent in July 2005.

These cases indicate that since the late 1990s, the courts have been more willing than legislatures to recognize homosexuals as deserving the same concern and respect as heterosexuals. It is very possible that the courts would not have extended rights to gays and lesbians if governments had been able to generate legally persuasive reasons as to why these rights should not be extended. The governments have been unable to do so. Not only have gays and lesbians won inclusion into social institutions because of court decisions (Smith 1999), but these decisions have likely also encouraged a higher level of participation of gays and lesbians in political institutions that have not been very accepting of their participation in the past (Scott 2001).

Native Rights

According to James Youngblood Henderson (1999, 393), "Colonization, in Canada, has systematically undermined the Aboriginal world view and justice system and created racism as the fundamental lens for viewing Aboriginal peoples." Many of Canada's Aboriginal peoples do not view the Canadian justice system as theirs. They did not help to develop it; it was imposed on them. And although the settler and Aboriginal communities share many values in common with regard to justice, Aboriginal communities place more emphasis on restorative justice and reconciliation. According to Henderson, because Aboriginal Canadians do not often identify with the Canadian justice system, the justice system is set up for failure among the Aboriginal population. This is one reason why a disproportionate number of Aboriginal people are convicted in criminal courts, are victims of crime, and are in our jails.

Mary Ellen Lafond (1999, 400), an Aboriginal judge in Saskatchewan, notes that in 1998 in that province, nearly 80 percent of those incarcerated in the Provincial Correctional Centre, 70 percent of those in the federal penitentiary system, and 95 percent of those in the young offenders' institutions were Aboriginal people, while the Aboriginal population in Saskatchewan was 13 percent (and expected to grow to 33 percent by 2020). She writes that "judges have a difficult task. We are imprisoned in a different sense ... When a large group of the population has little shared history and cultural symbols in the community it is impossible to appeal to common ground in sentencing an Aboriginal person" (401). And although the Criminal Code advises judges to "take into account all available sanctions other than imprisonment, for Aboriginal offenders" (s. 718.2(e)), she states that this section is little used because few alternatives are generally available, and non-Aboriginal lawyers may not be aware of those that are.

Canadian courts were not very open to participative or inclusive approaches regarding Native peoples until the early 1970s. Prior to that time, treaties were regarded as instruments that could be overridden at will by the federal and provincial governments, and Native bands with no treaties were entirely at the mercy of the federal and provincial authorities. Native perspectives on the meaning of treaties were given little weight, and the idea that Native groups that had not signed treaties (such as First Nations in British Columbia and the territories) retained aspects of sovereignty had no credibility in Canadian courts. This noninclusive view of Native rights began to change with the *Calder* decision of the Supreme Court in 1973 (*Calder* v. *British Columbia (A.G.)* 1973). The Nisga'a of northern British Columbia, who had never signed a treaty, claimed through litigation about a thousand square miles of land in the northwest of the province. When the case got to the Supreme Court of Canada, the Court was nearly evenly split. Three judges ruled that Aboriginal peoples have no legal entitlement to land claims. Three other judges, led by Mr. Justice Emmett Hall, held that Native title had not been extinguished. In the end, the Nisga'a lost on a technicality: the seventh judge ruled that from a procedural perspective, the Nisga'a cannot sue without Crown's permission. Nevertheless, the decision turned out to be a major step toward recognizing Aboriginal peoples as part of the Canadian polity. As well, it encouraged Aboriginal peoples as far away as Australia to begin to use the courts to try to obtain recognition denied them through the legislative process.

Thanks to the persistent pressure brought by Aboriginal peoples, the Constitution Act, 1982 included, in section 35(1), a guarantee that existing Aboriginal and treaty rights would be respected. This section gave additional ammunition to Aboriginal peoples in pursuing their rights claims through the courts. In the Supreme Court's decision in *R.* v. *Sparrow* (1990), the issue was whether an Aboriginal person fishing with a drift net over regulation size was exempt from those regulations because of commitments made in the Royal Proclamation of 1763. In the Royal Proclamation, the British Crown agreed to protect Aboriginal peoples from encroachments and harassment from settlers, and to protect traditional Aboriginal means of livelihood. The Crown argued that because governments had regulated the Aboriginal use of the fisheries for many years, any rights that the Aboriginal groups once possessed had demonstrably been extinguished. The Court disagreed. Aboriginal rights remained, the judges decreed, and were now protected from arbitrary reduction by section 35(1) of the Constitution Act, 1982. Regulation was not prohibited, but encroachments on Aboriginal rights had to conform to the fiduciary duty that the government owes to Aboriginal peoples. Among other things, if Aboriginal fishers are regulated, the government must demonstrate that Aboriginal rights have been interfered with as little as necessary to protect both Aboriginal rights and the fishery, that Aboriginal people have been consulted in the design of the regulations, and that they receive fair compensation for any fishing rights that have been validly limited.

In *Delgamuukw* v. *British Columbia* (1997), the issue was 58,000 square kilometres of land in northern British Columbia that was claimed by the Gitksan and Wet'suwet'en First Nations. This case dealt squarely with the questions of what Aboriginal title is protected by section 35(1), whether Aboriginal title had been extinguished after the passage of so many years with no treaty, and whether infringement of Aboriginal title is legally acceptable. The Supreme Court ruled that Aboriginal title can be seriously infringed only through a treaty-like negotiation between the government and the First Nation in question, and that any infringement of Aboriginal title requires full consultation. First Nations with no treaties have title to land that their ancestors traditionally occupied, where land use has been intensive. The First Nations have usufructuary (use) rights over lands less intensively occupied in the past. They have an obligation, however, to continue to use their lands in a way that is not "irreconcilable with the nature of the group's attachment to the land" (para. 117). First Nations that want to use their land in a nontraditional way must first negotiate surrender of the land to the federal government, which would then transfer the land to the First Nation as a reserve or private property. Traditional First Nations lands could not be interfered with except when there is a pressing need, and then there must be real consultation with the Aboriginal peoples and fair compensation.

The *Marshall* decision of 1999, which recognized Aboriginal fishing rights on the east coast based on treaties dating from 1760, has already been described in Chapter 2. The Supreme Court decided that Aboriginal fishing rights remained in existence, and that the federal government must take into account the special Aboriginal fishing rights when regulating the east coast fishery. This decision was interpreted very differently by the Mi'kmaq and by the non-Native fishers in Nova Scotia and New Brunswick. Some Native fishers completely ignored federal regulations regarding all types of fishing, while the non-Native fishers and federal officials emphasized the part of the Supreme Court decision that affirmed the federal government's right to regulate Native fishing. In November 1999, in the course of dismissing an application by the West Nova Fishermen's Coalition for a rehearing of the appeal, the Supreme Court attempted to clarify the September *Marshall* decision by emphasizing the right of the federal government to regulate the fishery. At the time of writing, however, the controversy between Native and non-Native fishers remains unresolved. Perhaps the turmoil resulting from the *Marshall* decision is a symptom of the upheavals that almost inevitably must take place when a society begins to attempt to include a group that has been excluded from fair participation in the justice system for so many years.

Have the Courts Gone too Far?

Some argue that the courts have intruded too much on the Canadian political process, particularly since 1982, by striking down legislation, interpreting principles such as judicial independence too unpredictably, and setting conditions for federal and provincial laws to comply with the Charter of Rights that are more a reflection of judicial discretion than the law (Morton and Knopff 2000). For example, there are valid reasons for disenfranchising all prisoners as part of the punishment for offending the norms of a democratic society, just as there are also valid reasons for enfranchising prisoners to promote rehabilitation and the valuing of the privileges of democracy. The argument is not that the courts are wrong in how they have resolved such issues, but that the proper forum for resolving these controversies – which do not have one right answer – is elected legislatures that respond to public opinion and the results of public debates. Would Canadian democracy be better off if the courts had interpreted the Charter, and the Constitution in general, in a restrained manner so as to have had minimal impact on public policy? Some leaders of the Conservative party have argued, for example, that only persons likely to interpret the Charter in a restrained fashion should be appointed. Such an approach would surely "politicize" the judicial appointments process.

The argument that the courts have been too activist in dealing with controversial public policy issues has a number of weaknesses. First, if the courts interpret the Charter conservatively so as not to disturb existing policy, future changes of policy may become more difficult. For example, if the courts had decided that the disenfranchisement of all prisoners, no matter how short their prison sentence, is not a Charter violation, it might have become difficult for future governments to change the policy to enfranchise prisoners serving short terms. It might be argued successfully in court that giving any prisoners the right to vote is contrary to the Charter, because giving persons previously considered unqualified to vote the franchise waters down the equal right to vote of law-abiding citizens. As well, once the Court has given its stamp of approval to a narrow interpretation of a right, this juristocratic approval has a tendency to be viewed as the "correct" interpretation, rather than a minimal interpretation of rights that can be enhanced by a willing legislature. A safer strategy is for the courts to give the Charter the "broad and liberal" interpretation advocated by Chief Justice Dickson (*R.* v. *Big M Drug Mart Ltd.* 1985, 305), and encourage legislatures to use the section 33 override to get around decisions they consider flagrantly misguided.

Second, courts cannot easily refuse to decide controversial issues that come before them, and leave them for elected legislatures. Canada's rules of justiciability, which define what questions can be decided in a court of law, mostly predate the Charter and are quite broad. So even if the courts decided to narrow those rules, it would take quite a few years, and very strong reasons, to reverse existing precedents (Sossin 1999). Even if a conservative federal government were to succeed in appointing a majority of judges sworn to judicial restraint, it would be improper from the perspective of common law and judicial independence for these judges to overrule precedents in a wholesale fashion in order to serve the wishes of their political masters.

Third, the public debate in Canada leading up to the establishment of the Charter generally favoured the judiciary taking an activist role in interpreting the Charter, and the Canadian public remains largely satisfied with the role that the Court has taken (Centre for Research and Information on Canada 2002; Fletcher and Howe 2000). By intervening to advance human rights principles, the judiciary is doing what most Canadians seem to want. As well, it should never be forgotten that the Supreme Court's approach to Charter jurisprudence could, at best, be described as mildly activist. Judges tend to have a conservative disposition, and as the cases reviewed in this chapter indicate, the Court's approach could hardly be described as radically interventionist.

Fourth, many elected politicians appear to be quite content to let the judiciary decide some controversial issues. When politicians take stands on divisive public issues, they often lose more support than they gain. After the decision of the Ontario Superior Court in July 2002 that the denial of opportunity for same-sex marriages is a violation of the Charter, the federal minister of justice, Martin Cauchon, announced that the government would appeal the decision. His announcement, however, was neither a defence of the principle that the institution of marriage ought to be restricted to heterosexuals, nor an occasion to express hope that the higher courts would give the stamp of approval to same-sex marriages. He sat on the fence, and explained the need for the courts to clarify public policy in this area (Simpson 2002).

Fifth, various groups have chosen to take issues about participation and inclusiveness to court rather than the legislature. Sometimes these groups think they will get a fairer hearing in court. Or, if an issue is not at the top of the government's policy agenda, they fear it is not likely to be dealt with through legislative action in a timely fashion.

Finally, as the review of cases in this chapter has shown, the record of the Supreme Court of Canada since 1982 demonstrates that the Court is open to reasoned arguments that could result in decisions that advance the cause of democratic principles such as equality, freedom from unjustified state intervention, inclusiveness, and participation. As has been stressed in this volume and others in the Democratic Audit series, democracy means a great deal more than majority rule, which can sometimes degenerate into unspeakable violations of human rights. Democracy is based on the belief that every member of society counts, deserves equal concern and respect, and in turn has obligations to democratic institutions to enable them to work. In other words, democracy is about inclusiveness and participation, and democratic institutions must be responsive to the legitimate needs of citizens and to basic democratic values.

I leave it to readers to judge precisely how responsive the courts have been to the values of inclusiveness and participation. Clearly, however, a number of decisions have opened the door to higher levels of inclusiveness and participation in the Canadian political system, although it will be up to individual Canadians to utilize the possibilities opened by the courts.

Then again, it is disturbing in a democratic polity that so many citizens would prefer to have issues related to participation and inclusiveness decided by courts rather than by elected legislatures, because they perceive the courts as more likely to give them a fair hearing. There would be many benefits to having these kinds of issues debated and resolved more frequently through the political process, and the public debate that surrounds it, than through the courts. Public debate can have an educative effect, allowing misinformation created by such factors as stereotyping to be challenged. As well, we all benefit from the mental exercise of thinking about how democratic principles should be applied in practice. And there is the opportunity for the development of a civic pride in the public deliberative process, which reinforces the democratic spirit of a nation.

Even in the best of political conditions, it is unlikely that those seeking higher levels of inclusiveness and participation will stop using courts to pursue their objectives, or that judges will become significantly less activist in applying the Charter. There is no reason, however, why public policy issues with Charter implications cannot be tackled through both legislative activity and the legal process. As Janet

Hiebert (1999) has argued in relation to the *Mills* decision, when parliamentarians decide to investigate human rights issues comprehensively and fairly, the Supreme Court is willing to defer to Parliament's judgment. My interviews with appellate judges in the 1990s taught me that most judges would welcome more legislative involvement in determining complex human rights issues; many judges are activist because elected representatives are reticent to tackle difficult rights issues (Greene et al. 1998).

In order to encourage legislatures to be more involved in determining controversial human rights issues, what is needed is political leadership willing to confront controversial rights questions by encouraging informed public debate and subsequently taking principled positions. From this perspective, it would have made sense for Justice Minister Cauchon, instead of taking no position on the issue of gay marriage, to have set out what he considered to be the pros and cons of sanctioning gay marriage. After acknowledging that public opinion polls showed that Canadians were about evenly split on the issue, he could have announced that he would be watching the public debate on the issue, would welcome letters on the subject, and after several months would announce government policy in this area. Clearly, the justice minister could not take a position without the blessing of the cabinet and especially the prime minister. But without governments that are willing to encourage public debate and then take a stand that they are willing to defend in court, the resolution of these kinds of issues is transferred from legislatures to lawyers, public interest groups, and judges. This situation is not the fault of the courts but the result of timid political leadership.

Chapter 5

Strengths

♦ Since the Charter of Rights came into effect, the Supreme Court of Canada has generally shown a remarkable ability (compared with much of its pre-Charter jurisprudence) to apply the Charter of Rights consistently with the basic principles of Canadian democracy.

♦ Dissenting opinions regarding contentious human rights issues provide grist for the mill of continued public debate.

♦ To the extent that there is a dialogue between courts and legislatures, Supreme Court decisions do not close the debate on contentious issues, but enrich it.

♦ Litigation provides a way in which the grievances and aspirations of Canadian citizens who have felt marginalized in the past can have an impact on public policy.

Weaknesses

♦ The Supreme Court might get too far ahead of public opinion in extending principles of human rights (prisoners' voting rights and gay marriage being cases in point), thus eroding its credibility and the credibility of the Charter.

♦ Because of the cost of litigation, and the haphazard way in which particular groups decide to litigate or intervene, important ideas from certain segments of society are sometimes not represented in court.

♦ The high stakes of some Charter litigation may cause the appointments process for the Supreme Court and lower courts to become highly politicized, resulting in a less balanced and fair judiciary.

♦ Legal issues tend to be narrow in scope, and therefore legal decisions sometimes make for bad public policy.

♦ It may be easier for narrow special interest groups to "capture" the litigation process than the legislative process.

6 THE COURTS AND DEMOCRACY

This book has presented an evaluation of Canadian courts according to the democratic benchmarks of participation, inclusiveness, and responsiveness. This analysis is unorthodox from two perspectives. First, the usual debate about the courts and democracy centres on whether judges ought to make decisions that affect policy matters – matters supposedly under the exclusive purview of elected legislatures. In contrast, I take the position that judges always have and always will make decisions that affect policy. As long as judges stay within the bounds of jurisprudential principles, these policy-related decisions are an important part of the democratic process. The central question is to what extent these decisions promote democratic values such as inclusiveness and participation.

Second, in addition to considering issues surrounding judicial decision making, I believe that in order to evaluate courts properly we ought to be asking questions about their nature as key institutions in a democratic polity. For example, how inclusive are the courts in terms of representing the various ethnic and demographic groups in Canadian society? To what degree do the courts as institutions facilitate appropriate public participation? And how responsive are the courts to the public demand for a fair, impartial, and expeditious dispute-resolution service? These institutional questions are just as important as the content of judicial decisions in evaluating the contribution of courts to Canadian democracy.

This concluding chapter provides my own commentary on the current state of the Canadian court system under the headings of participation, inclusiveness, institutional responsiveness, and decision-making responsiveness. I compare Canadian courts to courts in other liberal democracies rather than to a standard of absolute perfection, and I consider whether salient issues are being addressed or ignored. Most importantly, I list some avenues for reform that I hope will make the Canadian court system more participatory, inclusive, and responsive.

First of all, however, it would be useful to revisit the relationships between courts and the other two branches of government, the executive and legislature.

The Democratic Triangle: Courts, Legislatures, and Executives

It has been two and a half centuries since Montesquieu made the claim that a separation of powers between courts, executives, and legislatures in the United Kingdom ensured that each branch of government acted as a check on the other two, thus preventing tyranny and promoting liberty (Montesquieu [1748] 1989). What was intended to be a description eventually became prescription. So it became assumed in democracies that judges ought not to "make" the law because that function is the exclusive preserve of the legislative branch; judges ought not to administer courts because that function is the exclusive preserve of the executive; and neither the executive nor the legislature should attempt to interfere with the adjudicative process because that is the exclusive preserve of judges.

While Montesquieu's observations contain much wisdom, as a prescriptive tool they are too simplistic. The law can never be entirely clear, and so judges necessarily have a law-clarification role that is tantamount to a limited legislative function. Leaving court administration exclusively in the hands of the executive leaves open too many opportunities for cabinet ministers or public servants to interfere unfairly in the adjudicative process, and so judges need to control, at the very least, those aspects of court administration that directly affect adjudication (*Valente* v. *The Queen* 1985). And although judges in a democracy need to act as impartially as possible, and therefore must possess independence from the executive and legislative branches, the courts also need to be accountable in appropriate ways for the quality of the work they are expected to perform on behalf of our democracy. Although most of us think of accountability as being subject to the direction of a higher authority, the essence of accountability is the ability to demonstrate publicly the quality of one's work, and this is the sense in which I use the term.

The problem that some left- and right-wing critics of the Canadian judiciary have with many of Canada's judges is that they are too "activist," in the sense that they have a tendency to substitute their own policy judgments for those of an elected legislature. These critics see this tendency as both antidemocratic and a violation of judicial impartiality. But these critics seem motivated to criticize the judiciary only when a court makes a decision that they disagree with. For example, during the 2004 federal election, Stephen Harper, leader of the Conservative Party, vehemently criticized activist judges and vowed that if he became prime minister, he would appoint judges who respected the will of elected legislatures. In his earlier role as head of the right-wing lobby group the National Citizens Coalition (NCC), however, he was not critical of the Alberta Court of Queen's Bench for striking down part of the Canada Elections Act prohibiting third-party advertising. In fact, the invitation to the court to strike down the third-party advertising provisions had been brought by none other than the NCC. And when the revised third-party rules were upheld by the Supreme Court in 2004 in a case that Harper himself initiated so as to get the rules struck down, Harper certainly did not praise the Court for upholding the will of Parliament (*Harper* v. *Canada (A.G.)* 2004).

Clearly, courts cannot stray from applying the law as written whenever the law is clear. When the law is not clear, however, or when there is an apparent contradiction between the Constitution and a lower-level law, judges cannot help but be "activist," in the sense that they need to decide the issue and that decision will affect public policy. What is important, then, is the extent to which these discretionary decisions advance democracy.

Interesting though the judicial activism debate is, let's not forget the primary purpose of courts: to resolve legal disputes according to law, fairly, impartially, and expeditiously. Courts need to be responsive to the democratic imperative that they fulfill this purpose to the highest standard, and they need to demonstrate that they are doing so. Because the courts are central institutions in our democracy, they must also be open to appropriate public participation, and as institutions must reflect the demographic characteristics of our society.

Participation

Turning first to the issue of public participation in the Canadian court system, Chapter 2 outlined several ways in which the Canadian public can appropriately participate: involvement in judicial selection, in court administration, as litigants or witnesses, as members of juries, through public interest group litigation, or through expert witness testimony. We saw that although some progress has been made, public involvement in judicial selection and in court administration is currently much more limited than it ought to be in a democracy. A great many judges and lawyers still hold the view that lay persons have little if anything to contribute either to judicial selection or court administration. Two factors will result in change: a realization on the part of the public that the courts are there to serve the public interest, and that Canadians therefore have a right and duty to have input, and courageous leadership on the part of democratically minded attorneys general.

Members of the public have ample opportunity to participate as litigants and witnesses, although effective participation is often hampered by unnecessary delays and adjournments. As well, cross-examinations of litigants and witnesses are sometimes unnecessarily demeaning, thus discouraging participation because of the desire to avoid the ordeal. Innocent accused persons have been known to plead guilty to minor offences just to get the court process over with, and witnesses sometimes find excuses to avoid appearing in court.

The time may have come to investigate whether the trial system in criminal and civil courts, together with the adversary system, constitutes the fairest and most effective means of determining the facts. Some civil law countries, such as the Netherlands, seem to manage quite nicely without trials. Instead, the evidence is assembled by both sides and filed with the judge, who may conduct his or her own investigations. Hearings are held before the judge when necessary regarding particular facts or points of law, but it is not necessary to bring all the witnesses, litigants, and counsel together at the same time before the judge. I am not arguing that this system would necessarily work better in Canada, but only that there may be more effective ways of proceeding with litigation that could result in less inconvenience to litigants and witnesses, and fairer results. In some provinces, the rules in civil cases allow the examination in chief and cross-examination of expert witnesses before certified examiners, and the transcript is filed with the court. This procedure makes it a great deal easier to schedule trials, and is much more convenient for the experts. Might similar procedures be utilized in some kinds of criminal cases? What is called for is government-funded research into the entire litigation process to determine how it could be made more fair and effective.

The right to a trial by jury for serious criminal matters and some civil matters has always been a hallmark of public involvement in the courts. If the jury system is to retain its legitimacy, however, steps need to be taken to ensure that jurors are not treated simply as tools in the arsenals of clever counsel who may wish to use jury trials to delay, to force a settlement in civil suits because of the added expense, or to evade justice through manipulating the jury-selection system. The jury system was developed in the Middle Ages, when current knowledge about the selection of representative samples of populations did not exist. That knowledge could be used to choose juries that more truly represent the talents, skills, and backgrounds of Canadians in particular court districts. An improved process would offer less reason for challenges and objections to randomly selected jurors, and these could become the rare exception instead of the rule. Juries that are truly randomly selected would be less likely to be misused by counsel, and more likely to be used for their intended purpose – to provide a fair assessment by the litigant's peers.

Opportunities for participation through public interest group litigation and expert witness testimony are quite extensive in Canada, thanks to liberal rules of standing and the willingness of Canadian courts to consider social science and historical evidence. But a number of issues need to be addressed. First, the adversary system cannot always be relied on to ensure that all the relevant evidence is presented. In civil law countries, judges can conduct their own investigations, and this system seems to result in greater fairness in some situations. Is there a way in which Canadian judges could conduct their own research in cases where they are not satisfied with the extent of the evidence before them, while leaving this judicially collected evidence open to examination and rebuttal by the litigating parties? Second, as cases like *Marshall, Askov,* and *Morin* have illustrated, neither judges nor lawyers are as skilled as they might be in utilizing social science and historical evidence effectively. Third, social scientists and historians often lack the skills needed to present their evidence in a way that can be clearly understood and effectively used by lawyers and judges. Clearly, more educational opportunities need to be provided to lawyers and judges about the use of social science and historical evidence, and social scientists and historians would benefit from an orientation regarding how to present their evidence in a fashion that is as useful as possible to the court.

Inclusiveness

Canadian courts are indeed responding to the democratic need to be inclusive of Canadians of all ethnic and social backgrounds, and to be inclusive of women. As well, they are responding, to some extent, to the need to provide access to justice to all, regardless of social background.

Although lawyers and other legal professionals are not part of the court system per se, we have taken a look at their backgrounds because judges are drawn from among the ranks of lawyers, and because the backgrounds of lawyers and paralegals affect the nature of the involvement of ordinary Canadians in the justice system. Most Canadian law schools are making tangible efforts to encourage women, visible minorities, Aboriginal Canadians, and economically disadvantaged Canadians to enter the legal profession. As a result, women now constitute about a third of Canadian lawyers, and half of the current graduates of a number of law schools. Four-fifths of Canadian paralegals are women, however, as are virtually all legal secretaries, indicating that men still tend to dominate the top echelons of the legal profession (lawyers). Aboriginal peoples are seriously underrepresented in the legal professions, although their current participation rate is a vast improvement since the mid-twentieth century, when there were virtually no Aboriginal people in the legal professions. There would need to be four times as many Aboriginal lawyers as there are now, and three times as many Aboriginal paralegals, for these populations to hold a representative proportion of the legal professions. Visible minorities and immigrants are nearly equitably represented among paralegals and legal secretaries, but their numbers would need to double among lawyers to achieve equitable representation. The proportion of visible minorities and Aboriginal Canadians entering the legal profession is increasing. The fact that the legal profession is becoming more representative of the demographic groups in Canadian society means not only that Canadians who need lawyers will have greater choice, but also that a broader spectrum of lawyers is available for judicial selection.

An examination of the backgrounds of Canadian judges shows, understandably, that the judges tend to exhibit the same demographic characteristics as lawyers, though lagging a little behind the demographic changes that have occurred among the lawyers. About a quarter of Canadian judges are now women, which is a higher proportion of women than in most Canadian legislatures. As with lawyers, we would need to have four times as many judges of Aboriginal descent than we currently have for equitable Aboriginal representation among

Canadian judges. As well, it is likely that new Canadians, including visible minorities, are underrepresented in the Canadian judiciary, although the situation is improving.

Do Canadians of all backgrounds have an equal opportunity to work in the courts? Among court support staff, women constitute two-fifths of the administrative positions, four-fifths of the clerks, and more than nine-tenths of the recorders and transcriptionists. Nearly all of the sheriffs and bailiffs are men, and women working in the courts in general earn significantly less than men. Thus although progress is being made to promote gender equity among lawyers and judges, among court support staff gender occupational stereotypes still predominate. In contrast, Aboriginal peoples are equitably represented among court support staff. And although visible minorities are underrepresented, they are not as underrepresented as they are among lawyers.

Concerning litigants, our legal aid system appears to ensure that very poor Canadians have legal representation in criminal cases, and in some civil cases, which guarantees a degree of equity regarding the inclusion benchmark. Major cuts to legal aid during the 1990s, however, and a reduction in the amount of pro bono work done by lawyers since the advent of legal aid, have increased the number of poor and middle-income Canadians who go to court unrepresented. Our system has not adequately responded to this challenge. Given the demand for increasing public expenditures in the areas of health care and education, legal aid budgets are not likely to increase. But better services could be provided, and in a cost-effective way, to those who cannot afford lawyers by expanding the scope of services provided by community legal clinics. This is an option that some powerful interests in the legal profession are bound to oppose because of the potential impact on their incomes, and so only persistent public pressure will result in the needed reforms.

As well, increasing numbers of Canadians are deciding to represent themselves in court even if they can afford a lawyer. Some Canadian courts and legal information services are responding creatively to this challenge by providing information about court procedures on the Internet, CDs, and videocassettes and DVDs. Making it increasingly possible to get access to the justice system without lawyers is good for democracy, where the services of lawyers are not really necessary. But where lawyers are truly necessary, the financial circumstances of litigants should not be an impediment. It would be useful to research the possibility of creating a legal insurance scheme that would be universal, portable, comprehensive, and sustainable – like Canadian health insurance was intended to be.

Institutional Responsiveness

Overall, how responsive are Canadian courts as institutions? Canadians expect their judges to be able to make decisions that are as impartial as possible after a fair hearing. Most Canadians are satisfied with the quality of judicial decision making, and Canadian courts have made important contributions to thinking about the nature of judicial independence and impartiality. The independence and qualifications of justices of the peace and members of administrative tribunals, however, are often overlooked because of our tendency to fixate on courts presided over by judges. When we look closely at JPs and administrative tribunals, we find too many examples of pure patronage appointments, lack of appropriate expertise, and lack of independence. Clearly, these deficiencies at the lower levels of adjudication need to be addressed with some urgency.

And although procedures for ensuring appointments based on merit rather than patronage have improved during the last half of the twentieth century, some work remains to be done. Particularly at the federal level, there is still too much room for political patronage in provincial superior court appointments. This much was acknowledged by federal justice minister Irwin Cotler in a 2004 media interview. He hinted that he would prefer a system of appointments that would result in the best judges regardless of their political persuasion, rather than the current system, which might simply screen out the worst of the patronage hopefuls (Makin 2004). The procedure for elevating judges to appeal courts also needs reform. At the moment, elevations from the lower courts to the appeal courts are left entirely to the discretion of the minister of justice and the prime minister, and a greater potential violation of judicial independence is hard to imagine. A selection committee system to recommend elevations, as recommended by Martin Friedland (1995), would be a welcome improvement.

The Martin government attempted to "democratize" the process for appointment of Supreme Court of Canada judges by making it more transparent, and by having the two appointments in 2004 ratified by an ad hoc committee consisting of seven MPs, a lawyer, and a judge. It is to be hoped that this interim arrangement will not become the permanent procedure, and that the government will consider striking a search committee for the Supreme Court whenever a vacancy occurs. Such a search committee might include several MPs from different parties, a nominee of the premier of the relevant province, a lawyer, a retired judge, and several nonlawyers selected to represent the public interest.

Systems for handling complaints about judges for inappropriate behaviour are fair and effective, although they may be underutilized because of a lack of public knowledge about where to lodge a complaint. Now that good systems are in place for handling complaints, the time may be right to think positively about improving judicial performance, rather than just negatively about dealing with problems. Evaluation systems for judges, as recommended by Friedland (1995), could be utilized by judges to constantly improve themselves, just as professors benefit from student evaluations.

With regard to expeditious justice, unnecessary delay has been a problem in courts from time immemorial. Delay can never be resolved once and for all, because it is not always in the best interests of all litigants to move a case along as expeditiously as possible. During the last three decades of the twentieth century, some Canadian courts made inroads to tackle unnecessary delays through diverting out of the courts cases that are not appropriate for adjudication. The techniques included mandatory and nonmandatory mediation, the use of case-flow management techniques by judges, the appointment of case management masters, and the creation of courts management committees to find solutions with the help of all interested parties. There is no cure-all for unnecessary delays, but appropriate leadership from the judiciary and the executive, together with proper research and data analysis, can often resolve seemingly intractable delay problems. Nevertheless, unless lawyers' codes of ethics are revised to prohibit the use of delay as a tactical weapon, the best strategies for delay reduction will always encounter serious roadblocks.

Decision-Making Responsiveness

As Chapter 5 showed, the Supreme Court and other Canadian courts have, in response to representations from litigants, applied the Charter so as to promote higher levels of inclusiveness and participation, though the courts could clearly have gone further in some cases. From my perspective, which is quite different from that of the left- and right-wing Charter critics, courts perform an integral role in a democracy by adjudicating disputes about the application of basic democratic values enshrined in the Constitution. Judicial decisions have resulted in the greater inclusion of visible minorities, the mentally and physically handicapped, gays and lesbians, and Aboriginal Canadians in Canadian political institutions. For decades before the Charter, Canadian judges sometimes stopped elected officials from abusing power. Since the Charter, Canadian judges have through their decisions promoted public debate and participation regarding a number of issues, and have encouraged legislatures to use their research potential to puzzle through democratically acceptable balances between conflicting rights. And the Supreme Court has provided a thoughtful analysis of the democratic considerations that would apply if a province indicated a desire to secede from Confederation. By and large, judicial decisions that have affected policy matters have advanced rather than retarded Canadian democracy.

Furthermore, there is no reason the courts should have the "last say" in these kinds of cases. In Canada, governments can use the section 33 override to set aside judicial interpretation of some of the key parts of the Charter of Rights. And as scholars such as Hogg and Thornton (1999) and Monahan (1987) have shown, governments can usually achieve their policy objectives while at the same time adhering to judicial interpretation of the Constitution. Finally, Canada's "aggregate legislature," the legislatures of seven provinces representing 50 percent of the population, together with the federal Parliament, has the ability to amend the Charter if they can't live with judicial interpretation of it. To limit the judicial role in democracy would be to limit democracy itself.

Overall, Canadian courts are doing very well in some areas, such as their contribution to independence and impartiality. But there is a great deal of room for improvement in other areas, such as public participation in court administration and judicial selection, responsiveness to problems of unnecessary delay, support for self-represented litigants, and the respectful treatment of juries, witnesses, and litigants. My hope in highlighting issues that deserve attention is that these issues will be taken more seriously by judges, lawyers, elected members, and the Canadian public as a whole.

Discussion Questions

Chapter 1: Canada's Courts in Context

1   What are the principal functions of courts in Canadian democracy?

2   Do democratic principles require any changes in the way that courts, which are very old institutions, function today?

3   How would you evaluate Canada's court system, and the joint responsibilities of the federal and provincial governments in running it? Is it good to have an essentially unitary court structure in a federal country, with each order of government assigned different functions? Or is it a recipe for confusion?

Chapter 2: Public Participation in the Justice System

1   What level of public participation should there be in judicial appointment procedures at all levels?

2   Does the open court concept promote public accountability, or does it needlessly embarrass innocent people?

3   What are the most appropriate ways to promote public participation in pointing out serious problems in administering the courts, and in finding solutions to these problems?

4   Are litigants and witnesses in Canadian courts treated with the respect owed to them in a democratic context?

5   Does the Canadian jury system need reform?

6   To what extent can members of the public participate in court proceedings through public interest groups, and through expert witnesses?

Chapter 3: Inclusiveness

1   To what extent should those who work as judges, lawyers, and court support staff reflect the demographic make-up of Canadian society?

2   Is it a concern that women are so overrepresented among paralegals, court reporters, and legal secretaries?

3   Is it a concern that Aboriginal Canadians, visible minorities, new Canadians, and women tend to earn less than their counterparts in the court system?

4   What can be done for Canadians who do not view the justice system as "their" system?

5   Should affirmative action programs be established to help remove systemic barriers to employment for nontraditional groups in the justice system?

6   Given that society's financial resources are not unlimited, and that there are great needs for increased funding for health care and education, how should we determine a fair level of funding for legal aid?

Chapter 4: Responsiveness of Courts to Expectations
1   Is judicial independence in Canada in danger among judges, justices of the peace, or members of administrative tribunals?
2   Would greater judicial control over court administration promote judicial independence, or threaten it?
3   What are the most important contributions that Canadian judicial decisions have made to our understanding judicial independence in a democracy?
4   Are Canadian judges doing a good job of disciplining themselves?
5   Should judges, like professors, be evaluated on their fairness in overseeing courtroom procedures?
6   What would reduce the incidence of unnecessary delays in litigation?

Chapter 5: Responsiveness of Judicial Decisions to Canadian Democracy
1   Why do the left- and right-wing critics of judicial activism interpret the impact of the same judicial decisions in such different ways?
2   Is there a real "dialogue" between courts and legislatures about how the Charter should be interpreted?
3   Which Supreme Court decisions have advanced Canadian democracy by promoting inclusiveness and participation?
4   Which Supreme Court decisions have retarded Canadian democracy by restricting, or failing to promote, inclusiveness and participation?
5   In a democratic context, do those who appear to be working contrary to democratic principles, such as hatemongers or terrorist supporters, need to be treated with respect?
6   What is the best strategy for groups wanting to change public policy to promote greater social equality, inclusiveness, and participation: working through litigation, lobbying our elected legislators, or both?

Additional Reading

Chapter 1: Canada's Courts in Context

A good basic introduction to Canada's court system is contained in Gerald Gall, *The Canadian legal system,* 5th ed. (2004). A comprehensive analysis of the history and issues in the court system is found in Peter Russell, *The judiciary in Canada: The third branch of government* (1987). Peter McCormick's 1995 book, *Canada's courts,* provides a social science analysis of Canada's court system and why it functions as it does. *Final appeal: Decision-making in Canadian courts of appeal* (1998), by Ian Greene et al., provides insights into how the provincial courts of appeal and the Supreme Court of Canada function, based on interviews with the judges in these courts and data from court files. With regard to trial courts, Peter McCormick's and my *Judges and judging: Inside the Canadian judicial system* (1990) presents the results of interviews with trial court judges in Alberta and Ontario about judicial decision making.

Chapter 2: Public Participation in the Justice System

Martin Friedland's 1995 study, commissioned by the Canadian Judicial Council, *A place apart: Judicial independence and accountability in Canada,* is a comprehensive review of sticky issues in court administration related to independence and accountability. It is supportive of greater public input, as well as appropriate evaluation procedures for judges. Both the commissioner for federal judicial affairs and the various provincial ministries of the attorney general (Department of Justice in Quebec) maintain web sites describing how the judicial appointment process works, and how to apply for a judgeship. The study of the federal judicial appointments advisory committee system by Peter Russell and Jacob Ziegel, "Federal judicial appointments: An appraisal of the first Mulroney government's appointments and the new judicial advisory committees" (1991) shows how patronage can continue to play a major role in judicial appointments unless the appointments advisory system plays a recruitment role, and not just a screening function. Peter McCormick's analysis of the evolution of the Supreme Court after it became Canada's final court of appeal in 1949, *Supreme at last: The evolution of the Supreme Court of Canada* (2000), illustrates how courts evolve, in part in reaction to public expectations of their role. *Judicial administration in Canada* (1982) by Perry Millar and Carl Baar is the classic analysis of the tension between judge-centred and executive-centred approaches to court administration. The articles by Neil Vidmar, "The Canadian criminal jury: Searching for a middle ground" (1999), and W.A. Bogart, "Guardian of civil rights ... medieval relic: The civil jury in Canada" (1999), present a cogent analysis of the issues faced by the criminal and civil jury systems in Canada, respectively. The volume edited by Paul Howe and Peter H. Russell, *Judicial power and Canadian democracy* (2001), contains several articles that include empirical research on the attitudes of Canadians toward some recent important judicial decisions.

Chapter 3: Inclusiveness

Ellen Anderson's book, *Judging Bertha Wilson: Law as large as life* (2001), is a fascinating account of a woman's struggle to challenge the male-dominated law profession and judiciary. Two of Justice Wilson's publications provide useful insights into lawyering and judging from a woman's perspective: *Touchstones for change: Equality, diversity, and accountability* (1993) and "Will women judges really make a difference?" (1990). The Canadian Centre for Justice Statistics, a division of Statistics Canada, is a rich source both of data and of papers that analyze these data, such as Katie Snowball's *Courts resources, expenditures, and personnel, 2000/01* (2002) and Jean-Pierre Goudreau's *A statistical profile of persons working in justice-related professions in Canada, 1996* (2002). These, along with a continuing stream of up-to-date articles, are for sale on the Statistics Canada web site. Mary Ellen Lafond, an Aboriginal judge in Saskatchewan, provides an interesting commentary on the Aboriginal perspective on the justice system in "Justice for Aboriginals: Shared responsibility and accountability," which is published in *Justice to order* (1999), edited by Hélène Dumont and Gene-Anne Smith – a volume that contains several other articles about the Aboriginal perspective.

Chapter 4: Responsiveness of Courts to Expectations

The books by Martin Friedland, *A place apart: Judicial independence and accountability in Canada* (1995), and Peter Russell, *The judiciary in Canada: The third branch of government* (1987), are the two decisive works that provide the necessary background for the topics covered in this chapter. To keep up with the Supreme Court of Canada jurisprudence on judicial independence, consult the most recent edition of Peter Hogg's *Constitutional law of Canada* (2004). For summaries of investigations into the complaints made against federally appointed judges, see the annual reports of the Canadian Judicial Council, which can be purchased from the council's office in Ottawa or downloaded from the Council's web site, www.cjc-ccm.gc.ca. As well, the Canadian Judicial Council's publication *Ethical principles for judges* (1998) is an important blueprint for standards of judicial conduct. Statistics Canada is a good source for survey research into the attitudes of Canadians toward the justice system. The *Windsor Yearbook of Access to Justice* is one of the best sources of information about problems in justice system administration and attempted solutions to these problems.

Chapter 5: Responsiveness of Judicial Decisions to Canadian Democracy

The classic left-wing critique of judicial activism in Canada is Michael Mandel's *The Charter of Rights and the legalization of politics in Canada* (1994), while on the right, the two touchstones are *The Charter revolution and the court party* (2000) and *Charter politics* (1992), both by Rainer Knopff and F.L. Morton. In spite of his clear position on the right, Morton presents a balanced set of readings about various issues in Canadian law and politics in *Law, politics and the judicial process in Canada* (2002). Christopher Manfredi's *Judicial power and the Charter: Canada and the paradox of liberal constitutionalism*, 2nd ed. (2001) provides a comprehensive analysis of Charter politics, while Ran Hirschl's *Towards juristocracy* (2004) warns that in several Western democracies, activist judges and complacent politicians in a sense join forces to protect the status quo. Richard Sigurdson's article "Left- and right-wing Charterphobia in Canada" (1993) provides a well-deserved critique of some of the more extreme commentaries on judicial activism and the Charter. Janet Hiebert's book *Charter conflicts: What is Parliament's role?* (2002) shows how legislatures, executives, and courts all have a legitimate role to play in interpreting and applying the Charter. Finally, Peter Hogg and Allison Thornton's important article "The Charter dialogue between courts and legislatures" (1999) illustrates how the decisions of courts and legislatures might influence each other.

Works Cited

Cases

Andrews v. *Law Society of British Columbia*, [1989] 1 S.C.R. 143.

Beauregard v. *Canada*, [1986] 2 S.C.R. 56.

Bodner v. *Alberta*, [2005] S.C.R. 44.

Calder v. *British Columbia (A.G.)*, [1973] S.C.R. 313.

Delgamuukw v. *British Columbia*, [1997] 3 S.C.R. 1010.

Edwards v. *Canada (A.G.)*, [1930] A.C. 124.

EGALE Canada v. *Canada (A.G.)* (2003), 13 B.C.L.R. (4th) 1 (C.A.).

Eldridge v. *British Columbia (A.G.)*, [1997] 3 S.C.R. 624.

Ell v. *Alberta*, [2003] 1 S.C.R. 857.

Ford v. *Quebec (A.G.)*, [1988] 2 S.C.R. 712.

Halpern v. *Canada (A.G.)* (2003), 65 O.R. (3d) 161 (C.A.).

Harper v. *Canada (A.G.)*, [2004] 1 S.C.R. 827.

Hendricks v. *Quebec (A.G.)*, [2002] J.Q. 3816 (Sup. Ct.).

Landreville v. *The Queen*, [1973] F.C. 1223, 41 D.L.R. (3d) 574.

M. v. *H.*, [1999] 2 S.C.R. 3.

MacKeigan v. *Hickman*, [1989] 2 S.C.R. 796.

National Citizens Coalition v. *Canada (A.G.)*, [1984] 5 W.W.R. 436.

Newfoundland Assn. of Public Employees v. *R.* (2002), [2003] 220 Nfld. & P.E.I.R. 1.

OPSEU v. *Ontario (A.G.)*, [1987] 2 S.C.R. 2.

R. v. *Askov*, [1990] 2 S.C.R. 1199.

R. v. *Big M Drug Mart Ltd.*, [1985] 1 S.C.R. 295.

R. v. *Butler*, [1992] 1 S.C.R. 452.

R. v. *Edwards Books and Art Ltd.*, [1986] 2 S.C.R. 713.

R. v. *Keegstra*, [1990] 3 S.C.R. 697.

R. v. *Marshall*, [1999a] 3 S.C.R. 456 (17 September).

R. v. *Marshall*, [1999b] 3 S.C.R. 533 (17 November).

R. v. *Mills*, [1999] 3 S.C.R. 668.

R. v. *Morgentaler*, [1988] 1 S.C.R. 30.

R. v. *Morin*, [1992] 1 S.C.R. 771.

R. v. *Oakes*, [1986] 1 S.C.R. 103.

R. v. *O'Connor*, [1995] 4 S.C.R. 411.

R. v. *Sharpe*, [2001] 1 S.C.R. 45.

R. v. *Sioui*, [1990] 1 S.C.R. 1025.

R. v. *Sparrow,* [1990] 1 S.C.R. 1075.

R. v. *Zundel,* [1992] 2 S.C.R. 731.

Reference Re Anti-Inflation Act, [1976] 2 S.C.R. 373.

Reference re Alberta Statutes, [1938] S.C.R. 100.

Reference re Prov. Electoral Boundaries (Sask.), [1991] 2 S.C.R. 158.

Reference re Remuneration of Judges of the Provincial Court (P.E.I.), [1997] 3 S.C.R. 3.

Reference re Same-Sex Marriage, [2004] 3 S.C.R. 698.

Reference re Secession of Quebec, [1998] 2 S.C.R. 217.

RJR-MacDonald Inc. v. *Canada (A.G.),* [1995] 3 S.C.R. 199.

Robertson and Rosetanni v. *The Queen,* [1963] S.C.R. 651.

Rodriguez v. *British Columbia (A.G.),* [1993] 3 S.C.R. 519.

Roncarelli v. *Duplessis,* [1959] S.C.R. 121.

Sauvé v. *Canada (A.G.),* [1993] 2 S.C.R. 438.

Sauvé v. *Canada (Chief Electoral Officer),* [2002] 3 S.C.R. 519.

Schachter v. *Canada,* [1992] 2 S.C.R. 679.

Singh v. *Minister of Employment and Immigration,* [1985] 1 S.C.R. 177.

Switzman v. *Elbling and Quebec (A.G.),* [1957] S.C.R. 285.

Symes v. *Canada,* [1993] 4 S.C.R. 695.

Thibaudeau v. *Canada,* [1995] 2 S.C.R. 627.

Valente v. *The Queen,* [1985] 2 S.C.R. 673.

Vriend v. *Alberta,* [1998] 1 S.C.R. 493.

Statutes

Canadian Charter of Rights and Freedoms, Constitution Act, 1982, Schedule B to Canada Act 1982 (U.K.), Sections 1-34.

Constitution Act, 1867, U.K., 30 & 31 Victoria, c. 3.

Criminal Code, R.S.C., 1985, c. C-46.

Other Sources

Abraham, Henry J. 1998. *The judicial process: An introductory analysis of the courts of the United States, England and France,* 4th ed. New York: Oxford University Press.

Albo, Gregory, David Langille, and Lea Panitch. 1993. *A different kind of state? Popular power and democratic administration.* Toronto: Oxford University Press.

Anderson, Ellen. 2001. *Judging Bertha Wilson: Law as large as life.* Toronto: University of Toronto Press.

Armstrong, Jane. 2004. B.C. judge throws the book at sex-criminal colleague. *Globe and Mail,* 8 June, A1, A10.

Baar, Carl. 1975. *Separate but subservient: Court budgeting in the American states.* Lexington, MA: Lexington Books.

–. 1993. Criminal court delay and the Charter: The use and misuse of social facts in judicial policy making. *Canadian Bar Review* 72(3): 305-36.

Baar, Carl, Robert G. Hann, Lorne Sossin, Karim Benyekhlef, and Fabien Gelinas. 2005. *Canadian Judicial Council Project on Alternative Models of Court Administration.* Ottawa: Canadian Judicial Council.

Blackstone, William. [1769] 2001. *Commentaries on the laws of England.* Edited and with an introduction by Wayne Morrison. London: Cavendish.

Bogart, W.A. 1999. Guardian of civil rights ... medieval relic: The civil jury in Canada. *Law and Contemporary Problems* 62(2): 305-19.

Boldt, Menno, J. Anthony Long, and Leroy Little Bear. 1985. *The quest for justice: Aboriginal peoples and Aboriginal rights.* Toronto: University of Toronto Press.

Canadian Bar Association. 1985. *Report of the Canadian Bar Association committee on the appointment of judges in Canada.* Ottawa: Canadian Bar Association.

Canadian Judicial Council. 1998. *Ethical principles for judges.* Ottawa: Canadian Judicial Council.

–. 2002. *Annual report of the Canadian Judicial Council.* Ottawa: Canadian Judicial Council.

Centre for Research and Information on Canada. 2002. *The Charter: Dividing or uniting Canadians?* Montreal: Centre for Research and Information on Canada.

Chartrand, Paul L.A.H., Wendy Whitecloud, Eva McKay, and Doris Young. 2001. *Aboriginal Justice Implementation Commission Final Report.* Winnipeg: Statutory Publications Office.

Cooper, Cleve. 1999. Accommodation of the Aboriginal justice perspective by the Royal Canadian Mounted Police. In Dumont and Smith 1999, 417-30.

Cotler, Irwin. 2004a. Presentation to Justice Committee. Supreme Court of Canada Appointments Process. 30 March.

–. 2004b. Speaking notes for Irwin Cotler, Minister of Justice and Attorney General of Canada on the occasion of a presentation to the Ad Hoc Committee on Supreme Court of Canada Appointments. 25 August.

Daniels, Ronald J., Patrick Macklem, and Kent Roach. 2001. *The security of freedom: Essays on Canada's anti-terrorism bill.* Toronto: University of Toronto Press.

Dawson, John P. 1968. *The oracles of the law.* Ann Arbor: University of Michigan Law School.

Dawson, R. MacGregor. 1922. *The principle of official independence.* Toronto: S.B. Gundy.

Department of Justice. 1987. *Survey of public attitudes toward justice issues in Canada.* Toronto: Environics Research Group Limited.

Deschênes, Jules. 1981. *Maîtres chez eux: Une étude sur l'administration judiciaire autonome des tribunaux /Masters in their own house: A study on the independent judicial administration of the courts.* Ottawa: Canadian Judicial Council.

Docherty, David. 2005. *Legislatures.* Canadian Democratic Audit. Vancouver: UBC Press.

Doob, Anthony N., Patricia M. Baranek, and Susan M. Addario. 1991. *Understanding justices: A study of Canadian justices of the peace.* Toronto: Centre for Criminology, University of Toronto.

Dumont, Hélène, and Gene-Anne Smith, eds. 1999. *Justice to order: Adjustment to changing demands and co-ordination issues in the justice system in Canada, 1998.* Montreal: Éditions Thémis.

Dutil, Jean-L. 1999. A greater involvement ... a curb in crime. In Dumont and Smith 1999, 431-8.

Fletcher, Joseph F., and Paul Howe. 2000. *Public opinion and the courts.* Montreal: Institute for Research on Public Policy.

Friedland, Martin L. 1995. *A place apart: Judicial independence and accountability in Canada.* Ottawa: Canadian Judicial Council.

Galanter, Marc. 1974. Why the "haves" come out ahead: Speculations on the limits of legal change. *Law and Society Review* 9(1): 95-160.

Gall, Gerald L. 2004. *The Canadian legal system,* 5th ed. Scarborough, ON: Carswell.

Gavigan, Shelley. 1992. Morgentaler and beyond: Abortion, reproduction, and the courts. In *The politics of abortion,* ed. Janine Brodie, Shelley A.M. Gavigan, and Jane Jenson, 117-46. Toronto: Oxford University Press.

Goudreau, Jean-Pierre. 2002. *A statistical profile of persons working in justice-related professions in Canada, 1996.* Ottawa: Canadian Centre for Justice Statistics, Statistics Canada.

Granger, Christopher. 1996. *The criminal jury trial in Canada.* Toronto: Carswell.

Greene, Ian. 1982. The politics of court administration in Ontario. *Windsor Yearbook of Access to Justice* 2: 124-51.

–. 1983. The politics of judicial administration: The Ontario case. PhD diss., University of Toronto.

Greene, Ian, Carl Baar, Peter McCormick, George Szablowski, and Martin Thomas. 1998. *Final appeal: Decision-making in Canadian courts of appeal.* Toronto: James Lorimer.

Greene, Ian, and David P. Shugarman. 1997. *Honest politics: Seeking integrity in Canadian public life.* Toronto: James Lorimer.

Hein, Gregory. 2000. Interest group litigation and Canadian democracy. *Choices* 6(2): 3-30.

Henderson, James [Sa'ke'j] Youngblood. 1999. Aboriginal choices: Suffering under a failed criminal justice system or creating an Aboriginal attorney general office. In Dumont and Smith 1999, 391-7.

Hiebert, Janet L. 1990. Fair elections and freedom of expression under the Charter: Should interest groups' election expenditures be limited? *Journal of Canadian Studies* 24(4): 72-97.

–. 1996. *Limiting rights: The dilemma of judicial review.* Montreal and Kingston: McGill-Queen's University Press.

–. 1999. Wrestling with rights: Judges, Parliament and the making of social policy. *Choices* 5(3): 3-35.

–. 2002. *Charter conflicts: What is Parliament's role?* Montreal and Kingston: McGill-Queen's University Press.

Hirschl, Ran. 2004. *Towards juristocracy.* Cambridge MA: Harvard University Press.

Hogg, Peter W. 2004. *Constitutional law of Canada: 2004.* Scarborough, ON: Carswell.

Hogg, Peter W., and Allison Thornton. 1999. The Charter dialogue between courts and legislatures. *Policy Options* 20(3): 19-22.

Holdsworth, W.S. 1903. *A history of English law.* London: Methuen.

Howe, Paul, and Peter H. Russell, eds. 2001. *Judicial power and Canadian democracy.* Montreal and Kingston: McGill-Queen's University Press for the Institute for Research on Public Policy.

Ignatieff, Michael. 2000. *The rights revolution.* Toronto: House of Anansi Press.

Jones, David Phillip, and Anne S. de Villars. 2004. *Principles of administrative law,* 4th ed. Scarborough, ON: Thomson Carswell.

Kaplan, William. 2004. *The secret trial: Brian Mulroney, Stevie Cameron and the public trust.* Montreal and Kingston: McGill-Queen's University Press.

Knopff, Rainer, and F.L. Morton. 1992. *Charter politics.* Toronto: Nelson.

Lafond, Mary Ellen. 1999. Justice for Aboriginals: Shared responsibility and accountability. In Dumont and Smith 1999, 399-404.

Lederman, W.R. 1956. The independence of the judiciary. *Canadian Bar Review* 34: 769-809, 1139-79.

Locke, John. [1690] 1980. *Second treatise of government.* Edited by C.B. Macpherson. Indianapolis: Hackett.

Lowe, Diana, and Mary Stratton, with Lily Tsui. 2004. Information, knowledge, and good communication practices: Some preliminary findings from the Civil Justice System and the Public project. *Canadian Forum on Civil Justice Newsletter* 7 (Summer): 3.

MacCharles, Tonda. 2004. Harper unveils plan to change judiciary. *Toronto Star,* 9 June, A6.

McCormick, Peter. 1995. *Canada's courts.* Toronto: James Lorimer.

–. 2000. *Supreme at last: The evolution of the Supreme Court of Canada.* Toronto: James Lorimer.

McCormick, Peter, and Ian Greene. 1990. *Judges and judging: Inside the Canadian judicial system.* Toronto: James Lorimer.

McRuer, James Chalmers. 1968. *Royal Commission inquiry into civil rights.* Toronto: Queen's Printer.

Makin, Kirk. 2003. McLachlin urges overhaul of criminal-justice system. *Globe and Mail,* 18 August, A7.

–. 2004. Cotler aims to revamp system for appointing judges. *Globe and Mail,* 11 October, A1.

Mancuso, Maureen, Michael Atkinson, André Blais, Ian Greene, and Neil Nevitte. 2006. *A question of ethics: Canadians speak out about their politicians.* Rev. ed. Toronto: Oxford University Press.

Mandel, Michael. 1994. *The Charter of Rights and the legalization of politics in Canada.* Toronto: Thompson Educational Publishing.

Manfredi, Christopher P. 2001. *Judicial power and the Charter: Canada and the paradox of liberal constitutionalism,* 2nd ed. Don Mills, ON: Oxford University Press.

Manitoba. Commission of Inquiry Regarding Thomas Sophonow. 2001. *The inquiry regarding Thomas Sophonow: The investigation, prosecution and consideration of entitlement to compensation.* Winnipeg: Department of Justice.

Mendelsohn, Matthew. 2003. Same-sex solitudes. *Globe and Mail,* 23 August, A21.

Millar, Perry, and Carl Baar. 1982. *Judicial administration in Canada.* Montreal and Kingston: McGill-Queen's University Press.

Monahan, Patrick. 1987. *Politics and the Constitution: The Charter, federalism and the Supreme Court of Canada.* Scarborough, ON: Carswell.

–. 2002. Presentation to the Osgoode Law School 5th annual Constitutional Cases Conference. Toronto, 12 April 2001.

Montesquieu, Charles de Secondat, Baron de. [1748] 1989. *The Spirit of the Laws.* Translated and edited by Anne M. Cohler, Basia Carolyn Miller, and Harold Samuel Stone. Cambridge and New York: Cambridge University Press.

Morton, F.L., ed. 2002. *Law, politics and the judicial process in Canada.* Calgary: University of Calgary Press.

Morton, F.L., and Rainer Knopff. 2000. *The Charter revolution and the court party.* Peterborough, ON: Broadview Press.

Newman, Stephen L. 2004. American and Canadian perspectives on hate speech and the limits of free expression. In *Constitutional politics in Canada and the*

United States, ed. Stephen L. Newman, 153-73. Albany: State University of New York Press.

Nova Scotia. 2004. *Self-represented litigants in Nova Scotia: Needs assessment study.* Halifax: Department of Justice, Court Services.

Office of the Commissioner for Federal Judicial Affairs. 2005. Federal judicial appointments process – Judicial advisory committees. <www.fja.gc.ca/jud_app/process3_e.html>. (18 June 2005).

Ontario. Ministry of the Attorney General. 1999-2000. *Court Statistics Annual Report.* Report no. A-26. Toronto: The Ministry.

Ontario Judicial Appointments Advisory Committee. 2004. Where do judges come from? <www.ontariocourts.on.ca/judicial_appointments>. (18 June 2005).

Plucknett, T.F.T. 1940. *A concise history of the common law,* 3rd ed. London: Butterworth.

Roach, Kent. 2003. *September 11: Consequences for Canada.* Montreal and Kingston: McGill-Queen's University Press.

Royal Commission on the Donald Marshall Jr. Prosecution. 1990. Halifax, NS: The Commission.

Russell, Peter H. 1975. Judicial power in Canada's political culture. In *Courts and trials: A multi-disciplinary approach,* ed. M.L. Friedland, 75-88. Toronto: University of Toronto Press.

–. 1987. *The judiciary in Canada: The third branch of government.* Toronto: McGraw-Hill Ryerson.

Russell, Peter H., and Jacob S. Ziegel. 1991. Federal judicial appointments: An appraisal of the first Mulroney government's appointments and the new judicial advisory committees. *University of Toronto Law Journal* 41(1): 4-37.

Scott, Ian. 2001. *To make a difference: A memoir.* With Neil McCormick. Toronto: Stoddart.

Shapiro, Martin M. 1981. *Courts, a comparative and political analysis.* Chicago: University of Chicago Press.

Sigurdson, Richard. 1993. Left- and right-wing Charterphobia in Canada: A critique of the critics. *International Journal of Canadian Studies* 7-8: 95-115.

Simpson, Jeffrey. 2002. How we allow judges to tell us what to do. *Globe and Mail,* 30 July, A13.

Smith, Miriam Catherine. 1999. *Lesbian and gay rights in Canada: Social movements and equality-seeking, 1971-1995.* Toronto: University of Toronto Press.

Sniderman, Paul M. 1975. *Personality and democratic politics.* Berkeley: University of California Press.

Snowball, Katie. 2002. *Courts personnel and expenditures, 2000/01.* Report 85-403-XIE. Ottawa: Canadian Centre for Justice Statistics, Statistics Canada.

Solomon, Maureen, and Douglas K. Somerlot. 2000. *Caseflow management in the trial court: Now and for the future.* Chicago: American Bar Association.

Sossin, Lorne M. 1999. *Boundaries of judicial review: The law of justiciability in Canada.* Scarborough, ON: Carswell.

Statistics Canada. 1999. Canadian Centre for Justice Statistics Profile Series. Catalogue no. 85F0033MIE. <www.statcan.ca>. (8 December 2005).

–. 2001. *Legal aid in Canada: Description and Operations.* Ottawa: Canadian Centre for Justice Statistics.

–. 2002. *Legal aid in Canada: Resources and Caseload Statistics, 2001-2.* Ottawa: Canadian Centre for Justice Statistics.

Stein, Janice Gross. 2002. *The cult of efficiency.* Toronto: House of Anansi Press.

Tufts, Jennifer. 2002. Public attitudes toward the criminal justice system. *Juristat* (Canadian Centre for Justice Statistics) 20(12).

Vidmar, Neil. 1999. The Canadian criminal jury: Searching for a middle ground. *Law and Contemporary Problems* 62(2): 141-72.

Wicken, William C. 2002. *Mi'kmaq treaties on trial: History, land, and Donald Marshall Junior.* Toronto: University of Toronto Press.

Wilson, Bertha. 1990. Will women judges really make a difference? *Osgoode Hall Law Journal* 28(3): 507-22.

–. 1993. *Touchstones for change: Equality, diversity and accountability.* Report of the Canadian Bar Association task force on gender equality in the legal profession. Ottawa: Canadian Bar Association.

Young, Lisa, and Joanna Everitt. 2004. *Advocacy groups.* Canadian Democratic Audit. Vancouver: UBC Press.

Ziegel, Jacob S. 1999. Merit selection and democratization of appointments to the Supreme Court of Canada. *Choices* 5(2): 3-23.

Zuber, Thomas G. 1987. *Report of the Ontario Courts Inquiry.* Toronto: Ontario Ministry of the Attorney General.

Index

A master index to all volumes in the Canadian Democratic Audit series can be found at www.ubcpress.ca/readingroom/audit/index.